MEET ME AT THE MANGER...
AND
I'LL LEAD YOU TO THE CROSS

100 DAILY DEVOTIONS FROM CHRISTMAS TO EASTER FOR WOMEN

LEIGHANN McCOY

www.prayalltheway.com

The quoted ideas expressed in this book (but not Scripture verses) are not, in all cases, exact quotations, as some have been edited for clarity and brevity. In all cases, the author has attempted to maintain the speaker's original intent. In some cases, quoted material for this book was obtained from secondary sources, primarily print media. While every effort was made to ensure the accuracy of these sources, the accuracy cannot be guaranteed. For additions, deletions, corrections, or clarifications in future editions of this text, please write Leighann McCoy.

Unless otherwise stated all Scripture is The Holy Bible, New International Version®.(NIV) Copyright © 1973, 1978, 1984 International Bible Society. Used by permission of Zondervan. All rights reserved.

The Holy Bible, King James Version

The Holy Bible, New King James Version (NKJV) Copyright © 1982 by Thomas Nelson, Inc. Used by permission.

The Holman Christian Standard Bible™ (HCSB) Copyright © 1999, 2000, 2001 by Holman Bible Publishers. Used by permission.

The New American Standard Bible®, (NASB) Copyright © 1960, 1962, 1963, 1968, 1971, 1972, 1973, 1975, 1977, 1995 by The Lockman Foundation. Used by permission.

Cover Design by Kim Russell / Wahoo Designs
Page Layout by Bart Dawson

ISBN 978-1-60587-172-1

Printed in the United States of America

MEET ME AT THE MANGER...
AND
I'LL LEAD YOU
TO THE CROSS

100 DAILY DEVOTIONS
FROM CHRISTMAS TO EASTER
FOR WOMEN

LEIGHANN McCOY

TABLE OF CONTENTS

INTRODUCTION

Not knowing how to swim was a bit intimidating. While the other campers pushed and shoved their way to the dock's edge, I wiggled my toes in the sand and waited for the non-swimmers' relay, a foot race in the shallow edge of the lake. I loved the water but couldn't ever go where the action was. So, I spent most of my time that week making beaded key chains and decoupage boxes in the "craft hut." We were celebrating Christmas, and each of us surprised our "secret angel" daily with a tiny gift stuffed, her sock that dangled between springs at the foot of the metal bunk.

All week I was plagued with much more serious matters than my inability to swim. Outside of free time, camp consisted of Bible study, worship, cabin talks, and kitchen duty. I loved camp, but this was different. Ever since my counselor asked us to introduce ourselves and share our baptism story, I felt a discomfort that I couldn't escape. I had just finished sixth grade and was headed to a brand new middle school in the fall. And, I'd never been "baptized." Most of the other kids in my church had already made the courageous journey down the aisle to the front of the church. They'd been dunked. I knew I needed to do that, but since I'd waited so long, I was embarrassed; and the more I tried to talk myself into it, the more I resisted.

The Sunday before I left for camp I literally squeezed the pew in front of me to withstand the mysterious tug on my heart.

So when it came my turn to introduce myself to my cabin mates, I just left out the part that included when I was baptized. I felt like Dr. Seuss's sneetches. While it seemed to me all the other campers had "stars on thars," I didn't have a star on mine. They were in and I was out. They had it all together and they were swimming in the deep, while I was still slogging through the mud in a foot race on the shallow side of the dock.

Not only that, but the music leader seemed to especially enjoy a particularly popular youth tune (for the 1970s) that included this line, "Life was filled with guns and wars and everyone got trampled on the floor…I wish we'd all been ready. Two men traveled up a hill, one was gone and one was standing still…I wish we'd all been ready." The song referenced the moment in time when all believers might suddenly disappear and all the non-believers might find themselves "left behind." I knew the story, and I knew what separated me from them. They'd invited Jesus to live in their hearts and I hadn't. They'd settled the matter of where they would spend eternity and I hadn't. They were secure and I wasn't. They knew how to swim and I didn't.

So I tried to hide in the craft hut. But one night after dinner a missionary stood before us and sang "O Holy

Night." We were celebrating our Christmas Eve, and as he sang, I wandered toward the manger. In my mind, I left the dining hall and found myself surrounded not by a hundred pre-adolescent girls but by a donkey, a few sheep, some shepherds, a weary young woman, and a gentle man.

"…fall on your knees, and hear the angel's singing…"

But then the donkey, sheep, shepherds, Mary, and Joseph disappeared too; and as I made my way to the manger, I came face to face with a newborn baby. I lost myself in his eyes. But rather than touch the peach fuzz on his soft head, I was suddenly taken from that quiet place to a noisy hillside where people were shouting and the wind was howling. I forced myself to look up, and there I saw the same baby eyes look right into my soul as He hung dying on a splintered bloody cross.

That was when I heard Him say, "Leighann, if you had been the only one in the entire world who ever needed a Savior, I would have done this all for you. I would have come as a baby, lived a sinless life, and died a sinner's death so that you could come to Me. I love you…"

It was an invitation not a statement. He loved me so He wanted me. He wanted me to trust Him. He wanted me to invite Him in. He wanted me to get out of the mud, jump off the deep side of the dock, and trust Him to teach me to swim.

My immediate response was an overwhelming sorrow for what I did to Him. I was so sorry. The pain I felt was heavier than any guilt I'd ever experienced before. I did that to Him! I nailed Him there. Compelled by His love He embraced the cross for me! I cried. I didn't cry quiet tears; I cried from the depth of my 11-year-old soul. And as soon as my mind formed the words "I'm so sorry! Please forgive me!" the pain was replaced by peace. It wasn't simply a wiping away of grief but a washing away of fear, regret, insecurity, drudgery, and everything else that had separated me from the life I was created to live.

Even Jesus had a hard time explaining it to Nicodemus (John 3), and I'm not sure I'm doing it justice here, but I was born again. The old Leighann died that night at Camp Pinnacle in the North Georgia mountains, and the Leighann that was meant to be was born.

"...oh night, divine. Oh night when Christ had come. Oh night, divine! Oh night, oh holy night."

He met me at the manger and led me to the cross.

I know how to swim now. I'm a good swimmer in fact. I received my lifeguarding and water safety instructor certifications when I was in college and spent several years guarding pools and teaching others to swim. I've participated on swim teams and still swim today for exercise. I love the water.

I also know how to "swim" spiritually. I've learned to dive into His Word and breathe rhythmically with His promises. I often find myself in trouble that is over my head where His Spirit keeps me from drowning. If you'll let me, I'll try to allow Him to use these devotions to do the same for you.

Meet me at the manger,
and I'll lead you to the cross.

PART 1

MEET ME AT THE MANGER

*While they were there, the time came for the baby to be
born, and she gave birth to her firstborn, a son.
She wrapped him in cloths and placed him in a manger,
because there was no room for them in the inn.*

Luke 2:6-7

There was something different about those who
came to the manger that first holy night; something that allowed them to experience God's
work on the earth. While all the rest of the people were
going about their business, I wonder about the hearts of
those who came to the manger and experienced the first
Christmas.

*Father, open our eyes like You opened the eyes of the
shepherds—so that we can see the wonder of this child. Lord,
open our ears, like You opened the ears of Joseph—so that we
will be faithful with all the spiritual blessings You've entrusted
to us. Father, open our minds—like You opened the minds
of the wise men who traveled many days searching for truth.
And open our hearts—like You opened the heart of Mary so
that we might live our lives determined that "it be done to us…
as You have said." Amen*

CHAPTER 1

GETTING YOUR BEARINGS RIGHT

So Joseph also went up from the town of Nazareth
in Galilee to Judea, to Bethlehem the town of David,
because he belonged to the house and line of David.

Luke 2:4

I love nativity scenes and have lots of them; one is carved from olive wood. My husband Tom and I purchased it from a street vendor set up just outside the entrance to the Mount of Olives. In December 1995, I weaned my infant son TJ so I could travel to Israel with Tom. Alan Watson (an incredibly generous man who believed in us) invited us to go with him and his son on a tour of the Holy land just after Christmas. So we left our children with my parents in Georgia and boarded our flight to Amman, Jordan, where we traveled into Israel via the road to Jericho.

This trip was monumental for me. I cannot find the words to describe the wonder I sensed as I walked the streets, sat on the mountainsides, and sailed the waters. There was something surreal about walking where Jesus walked, sitting where Jesus sat, and sailing the same waters Jesus sailed. Although I *knew* Jesus lived and ministered on this earth—the stories maintained a sense of "fiction" to me until I was there. Because I grew up hearing the stories, and studying the maps, I was as familiar with my surroundings in Israel as I am when I visit my home state of Georgia. Because I'm from Marietta, Georgia, I know where the "big chicken" is, and I know how long it takes to get to a Braves game on Wednesday night after church. I know which roads lead me to my grandparents and which ones take me to Birmingham. I know how far I am from the mountains and how long it will take me to get to the beach.

Tennessee (my home for the past 20 years) also provides me with familiarity. I know how far it is to Cookeville on interstate 40 and to get off at exit 286 to take the back road to Starbucks. I know exactly where Bucksnort is in relationship to Dickson. I know that from my home in Franklin, I can be south of Atlanta before I can be to the tri-cities area, and that I can almost be across the great state of Kentucky before I can reach the tip where Virginia and Tennessee touch.

In the same way, before I went to Israel, I knew that the Dead Sea was near Jerusalem, that Bethlehem was south of Jerusalem, and that Nazareth was north. I knew that Capernaum and Bethsaida were on the shores of the Sea of Galilee, and that the Jordan River connected the two seas. I knew that these places really existed, and even envisioned what they looked like.

But to sit in the shade of the olive trees and watch the sunrise over the Sea of Galilee—to smell the fish and taste the bread…to dip water from the Jordan River and feel the wind in my face on the mountain where Jesus fed the 5,000—was to *know* by experience that God's Word is true!

MEET ME AT THE MANGER . . .

1. Have you ever visited the Holy Land? If so, jot down a few memories you have. If not, take a look at the maps in the back of your Bible. Place your finger on Bethlehem and say aloud, "This is a real place. Jesus was born right here."

2. Do you remember when you first heard the Christmas story? If you were too young to remember, thank God right now for a heritage of faith. If you can remember, thank God for getting the news to you.

3. What part of the Christmas story do you like best? What part is your least favorite?

PRAY THIS PRAYER: *Father, thank You for sending Jesus to a real world at a real time. Open my mind and my heart for this journey. Help me to absorb every tidbit of insight I'm about to discover, and bring this age-old story to life in me. In Jesus' name I pray. Amen*

CHAPTER 2

O LITTLE TOWN OF BETHLEHEM

*Bethlehem Ephrathah, you are small among
the clans of Judah; One will come from you to be
ruler over Israel for Me.*
Micah 5:2 HCSB

As Tom and I journeyed through the "promised land" we experienced many moments of wonder. But none compared with the experience I had when I stood near the spot where Jesus (supposedly) was born. This is what I wrote in my travel journal about that experience...

"Every day of our trip, I was overwhelmed at the reality of God's Word as we walked the streets Jesus walked. The maps in the back of my Bible represented real places. I recognized that the stories I've heard all my life are based on historical fact. They are not make-believe stories written, 'a long time ago in a faraway place.' But out of all the places we visited, the one that impacted me most was the cave where tradition says Mary and Joseph stayed the night Jesus was born.

We were in Bethlehem. The streets were lined with various shops. One was a butcher's shop—adorned with dead animals hanging in the windows. The flies swarmed around the meat. Another shop was a bakery where the smells of fresh bread offered a bit of sweet relief to the polluted air. We made our way through the busy streets to the Church of the Nativity (a Greek Orthodox church) and waited in an incense filled room for our turn to walk downstairs to a place in the basement area where Jesus was born.

Many of Israel's holy sites have been saved through the years by the construction of churches. Even in the midst of chaos in the Middle East, these sacred monuments provide some security to the holy sites. I determined early in my visit that the location of Jesus' miracles and milestones might not have been in the exact places our tour guide assured us they were. We also had to overlook what the tourist industry had added to their *exact locations* (they placed a plastic baby Jesus in a cradle in the cave at Bethlehem). But even if the exact location isn't known, and even if those locations have been enhanced with visuals, you can be sure that what they are showing you is at least a good representation of what might have been some 2000 years ago."

MEET ME AT THE MANGER . . .

1. Do you know the Christmas carol O *Little Town of Bethlehem*? Isn't it interesting that it has the phrase, "how still we see thee lie"? Do you think Bethlehem was still the night Jesus was born?

2. What would happen in your town if thousands of people suddenly came for a three-day event? Think about the busyness of Bethlehem the night Jesus was born. Some of God's most powerful activity takes place in the midst of chaos and goes unnoticed by the masses.

PRAY THIS PRAYER: *Lord, when I think of Bethlehem the night Jesus was born, I realize that the night was most likely not "silent." Instead it was filled with the noise of travelers visiting with distant relatives, vendors taking advantage of the opportunity, and no doubt many other activities that distracted people from You. I don't want to miss Your most powerful activity. Give me eyes to see You and ears to hear You even in the busyness of life so that I can know You today. Amen*

CHAPTER 3

THE WORD BECAME FLESH

The Word became flesh and dwelt among us,
and we have seen His glory, the glory of the One and Only,
who came from the Father, full of grace and truth.
John 1:14

A t the Church of the Nativity, the tour guides separated us into small groups of about 15 each. We waited turns going down the stairs to the basement through the layers of years that separated us from the birth of Jesus. The words of John 1:14 flooded my mind as I made my way down the stone steps.

"The Word became flesh and dwelt among us, and we have seen His glory, the glory of the One and Only, who came from the Father, full of grace and truth."

We stood in a semi-circle when we arrived at the opening. Under our feet was a cold dirt floor, and we were surrounded by stone walls. The air was cool and damp. The tour guide explained that stables in Jesus' day were not made out of wood (as they are portrayed in most of our nativity scenes), but that they were carved out of stone. I envisioned this "stable" filled with dirty animals and weary travelers. He then pointed to a gold plate on the floor that marked the (exact) spot where Jesus was born. My imagination carried me back to that first Christmas Eve. I could almost hear the hustle and bustle of people as they crowded into the city of David to be counted in the census. I could imagine the innkeeper looking at Joseph's desperate face and Mary's obvious pain. I could almost see Mary double over with the next wave of contractions as Joseph rushed to spread blankets on the hard floor.

And then, I stared at that gold plate. And I wondered at the majesty and love of God that would allow His Son to be born into this world. I wondered at the glory of God that would allow His Son to come to us since we were unable to go to Him. I worshipped God in that cave because I knew that had the Word not become flesh and dwelt among us, we could never have the opportunity to even begin to experience His glory. I thanked God for being full of grace and truth.

MEET ME AT THE MANGER . . .

1. Read John 1:1-14.

2. Consider what the true nativity most likely looked like. Consider the smells, the difficult time Mary must have had delivering Jesus in those surroundings and how God took care of her needs.

PRAY THIS PRAYER: *Thank You, Lord, for bringing Your Word to us in the Person of Jesus. Jesus, You were with God in the beginning; You are God. Through You all things were made. You are life and Your life is the light of men. Thank You for shining in my darkness.*

CHAPTER 4

IN THE BEGINNING

In the beginning was the Word,
and the Word was with God, and the Word was God.
He was with God in the beginning.

John 1:1-2

Think about that. Jesus, *the Word*, was with God in the very beginning. When God said, "Let us make man in our image, in our likeness…" (Genesis 1:26), *Us* referred to Him and Jesus (and the Holy Spirit).

Through Him all things were made; without him nothing was made that has been made. In him was life, and that life was the light of men. (John 1:4)

Jesus was with God when "He spoke the words and all the worlds came into order." He was in the hands and in the breath of God that…

…formed the man from the dust of the ground and breathed into his nostrils the breath of life, and the man became a living being. (Genesis 2:7)

And although Jesus gave all of us life when He breathed His life into us—and even though He came to earth to illumine our hearts and minds—not all of us understand this.

The light shines in the darkness, but the darkness has not understood it. (John 1.5)

I stood in the damp darkness of that cave and pondered that thought. Jesus, the Creator, the Life and the Light, came into the very world He created. He came to us in the helpless, fragile, earthly body of a tiny newborn infant.

The Word became flesh and dwelt among us. (John 1:14)

But not all of us beheld His glory.

He was in the world, and though the world was made through him, the world did not recognize him. He came to that which was his own, but his own did not receive him. (John 1:10-11)

How tragic. Jesus, the Creator, Giver and Light of Life, came to our world to bring us back to God. And those whom He loved chose the darkness over the light.

But not all of us chose the darkness.

Yet to all who received him, to those who believed in His name, He gave the right to become children of God—children born not of natural descent, nor of human decision or a husband's will, but born of God. (John 1:13)

And that is what we are! Children of God! All because…

The Word became flesh and dwelt among us. And we beheld His glory as the only begotten of the Father, full of grace and truth. (John 1:14 NASB)

MEET ME AT THE MANGER . . .

1. Compare John 1:1-14 that you read yesterday with Genesis 1 and Genesis 2:4-25.

2. Think of how great God's love was toward us "in the beginning" and then again when He sent His precious Word to "became flesh and dwell among us."

PRAY THIS PRAYER: *Father, thank You for loving me "in the beginning." Thank You for loving me by sending Your "Word to become flesh." Thank You for that holy night in that holy place. Lord, soak me in the depth of Your love as I ponder the wonder of the moment Jesus was born. Amen*

CHAPTER 5

THE FIGURES IN YOUR NATIVITY SCENES

*The Word became flesh and took up residence among us.
We observed His glory, the glory of the One and Only Son
from the Father, full of grace and truth.*

John 1:14 HCSB

In the nativity scene that the women's ministry team gave me a few years back I have these figurines: Mary, Joseph, baby Jesus, an angel, three incredibly clothed wise men, two shepherds, some sheep, camels, cattle, a few palm trees and a stable (made out of stone!). They all fit snuggly in a Styrofoam box (but you have to get them in just right—my set includes instructions on how to pack them after the season is over).

They represent those who attended Jesus' birthday party. We unpack them each year, and carefully place them all over our house—thinking of how amazing it might have been to *be there*. When my daughter Mikel was four or five, she rearranged my little scene. She put Jesus in the very center and surrounded Him with all the others. She had them circled up like covered wagons circled around their campfires. One year we took those wise men (who weren't actually *at* the stable the night Jesus was born) and led them on a journey. We started them at the top of the stairs and moved them down a step every day toward Christmas. It was a great way to re-live their journey to see Jesus.

But have you ever wondered, "why were they the only ones there?" I'm not talking about the wise men, but the shepherds, Mary, Joseph, the donkey, cow and sheep. Why were they the only ones there? I mean, Bethlehem was so full of people that "there was no room for them in the inn." Where was everybody else? Think of all the men, women, boys, and girls who were sleeping just next door—they totally missed the moment that changed forever.

While the entire world was gathered in Bethlehem that night—these are the only ones who came to the party. They were all invited, "For God so loved *THE WORLD*…," but these were the only ones who came.

MEET ME AT THE MANGER . . .

1. If you have your nativity scene nearby, take each figure in your hand and look carefully at that one. Consider the man or woman that it represents. Think of how Jesus' birth might have impacted their lives.

2. Who misses Christmas today? Why do they miss it? What can you do in your own home to make sure that your family members don't miss Christmas?

PRAY THIS PRAYER: *Father, I don't want to miss Christmas. I don't want my holiday season to be so full of tinsel and sugar that we forget who You are and why You came. Help me to think of ways I can make sure my family doesn't miss Christmas this year.*

CHAPTER 6

THE HUSTLE AND BUSTLE

In those days Caesar Augustus issued a decree that a census should be taken of the entire Roman world. (This was the first census that took place while Quirinius was governor of Syria.) And everyone went to his own town to register.

Luke 2:1-3

The rest of the people who traveled to Bethlehem for the census were caught up in the trappings of the event itself. A census of this magnitude didn't come around very often. Families who'd been separated for years were reunited as they traveled to the places of their births. Distant relatives gathered to share meals. Businessmen set up their stalls and took advantage of the opportunity to turn a profit. Drinks were shared, music filled the air, and children played in the streets. And in all the festivities, they missed Him. They missed the Christ-child. They missed the angels singing, and although they slept under the star's bright light, they never noticed how it illuminated the night.

The light shines in the darkness, but the darkness has not understood it. (John 1:5)

The moment that the "Word became flesh and dwelt among us" those within the sound of His voice never heard the voice of God when He cried in the night. They never gazed into His dark chocolate eyes, never counted His tiny toes or let Him grab their finger with his itty bitty hand. They didn't stroke the fuzz on his head or bow at His manger.

Most of the world went home when the party was over; they lived their lives the same as before; and they completely missed the DAY—the day the Glory of God became flesh and dwelt among us.

This year, most of the world will do the same. Christmas will come and Christmas will go. Families will reunite with one another and "survive" the time they spend together. Husbands will spend more than is reasonable on a "kiss that begins with K," and parents will go into debt to fill their children's wish lists. The retailers will set up their stalls, and fill our mailboxes with coupons taking full advantage of the opportunity to turn a profit. Drinks will be shared, music will fill the air, and children will fall into their beds exhausted from all the activities.

MEET ME AT THE MANGER . . .

1. But what about you? Will you join the "nativity scene"? Will you sense the wonder again this year?

2. Will you "keep watch" with the shepherds, "follow the star" with the wise men, and "sing" with the angels? Or will you let the moment pass you by?

PRAY THIS PRAYER: *Lord, forgive me for being distracted by chores during this time of the year. Forgive me for spending more time decorating my house and filling my social calendar than I spend alone with You reflecting on the holy moment we celebrate. I commit to You my worship and my love. I will not let this moment pass me by.*

CHAPTER 7

UP CLOSE AND PERSONAL

*But Mary treasured up all these things
and pondered them in her heart.*

Luke 2:19

For many years I didn't really miss it, but neither did I get it. I wasn't next to the manger—but perhaps standing far enough behind to peak around a shepherd.

I celebrated Christmas. When we drove by the "square" in downtown Marietta on our way to church, I rolled down my window so I could hear the music playing at the nativity scene that was there. I wore my blue skirt and white shirt, tied the little red bowtie and sang on the risers with my children's choir.

I remember one year when my sisters and I dressed in our PJs and sat on the steps of our church's altar while my dad read the Christmas story. (We supposedly portrayed a scene from our home. I only remember how awkward I felt having to wear my pajamas to church.) I watched as the lights were lit on the wreath that hung over the baptistery (indicating our progress toward the goal for giving to international missions). At home we sprinkled colored sugar on cookies and lit the advent candles. And my tummy played host to a million butterflies when I tried to sleep on Christmas Eve.

But the year I celebrated Christmas in July, I made my way from behind the shepherd and fearfully approached the manger. I'd gone to camp with a hundred other girls and only one that I knew. On the very first night our counselor asked us to introduce ourselves to the others. She said, "tell us where you go to church and when you were baptized." I'll never forget how terrified I was. Even though the cabin was dark and we were all nestled into our own bunks, I dreaded having to answer that simple question. I knew where I went to church, but I hadn't yet had the courage to be baptized there.

For several years the Holy Spirit had been inviting me to receive Jesus' gift of salvation, but I couldn't muster up the fortitude to actually unwrap His Presence. I knew that Jesus died for my sins and that He lived with God in heaven. I knew that in order to go there and live with Him when I died, I had to ask for His forgiveness and receive His gift of life. But, I also knew that inviting Jesus into my life meant giving Him permission to rule. And, I knew that when He took charge, the first thing He would want me to do would be to confess my faith in Him publicly—through baptism. That was where I resisted His gift. I simply could not walk to the front of my congregation, tell the pastor I wanted to follow Jesus, and

MEET ME AT THE MANGER · 39

let him baptize me. It was too much for a shy and insecure little girl.

So when it came my turn to introduce myself—I told them I attended First Baptist Church in Marietta, Georgia, and left it at that. Why did my counselor put us on the spot like that? I've put the pieces together now—my counselor asked us that question because she wanted to know who to pray for during the week we were in her care. My camp counselor was a college student who'd recently accepted Jesus' gift of salvation and she just hadn't gotten over it yet. She was convinced that God wanted to save every camper that slept under her roof. So she prayed for me the week I was sharing her space in the world.

MEET ME AT THE MANGER . . .

1. What is the difference between knowing about Christmas and experiencing Christmas?

2. Who did God use to bring you to Christ? What did he/she say that helped you make your decision?

3. Who have you helped lead to Christ?

PRAY THIS PRAYER: *Thank You, Lord, for [name of person who helped you know Christ]. I want to be that person for others. Give me "divine appointments" today—people with whom I can share You. Help me to be aware of what is going on in their hearts so that I might minister encouragement, hope, and life to them today. Amen*

CHAPTER 8

MEET ME AT THE MANGER

On coming to the house, they saw the child with his mother
Mary, and they bowed down and worshiped him…
Matthew 2:11

As part of our July Christmas celebration that summer at camp we hung socks on our beds, and our secret angels filled them with trinkets. We sang carols and listened to the Christmas story. On Thursday night a missionary sang "O Holy Night." And I found my way to the manger. While he sang the words, I listened. The Holy Spirit whispered to me (not audibly, more real than that), "Leighann, if you had been the only person in all the world who ever did anything wrong, I would have sent Jesus to lay in that manger."

I stepped forward from where I'd been hiding behind the shepherd's robes on the outskirts of the nativity that holy night. As I tentatively moved closer to the manger in my mind, God continued, "I would have brought Him to earth, He would have grown to be a man, live a sinless life and die on the cross for you."

I was actually sitting in the "mess hall" on cold metal chairs at recently wiped tables. But in my spirit, I touched the rough wood of the manger and wondered at the splinters that dug into Jesus' flesh on that "old rugged cross." The Holy Spirit didn't stop speaking to me, "Leighann, I sent My Son to die for you—for you. He bled and died because I love you! That baby in the manger…I gave Him to you."

As tears formed in my eyes, I knelt at the manger. I smelt the hay and heard the baby cry. Tears splashed on His swaddling clothes, and it was just me and Him— He opened His eyes and a smile formed on His face. He lifted His tiny little hand, and I gave Him my finger. He gripped it firm that night in the sanctuary of my mind at Camp Pinnacle in the North Georgia mountains and He has never let me go.

"Fall on your knees, and hear the angels singing. Oh Night, divine, oh night when Christ was born…"

"Forgive me, Lord! Forgive me for my sins that nailed You to the cross! Forgive me for resisting Your love! Oh God, I worship You! I give my life to You! Come into my heart! I want You!! Come into my heart oh God."

Have you been to the manger? Have you joined the figures in your nativity scene?

MEET ME AT THE MANGER . . .

1. Read Luke 2:1-7. Imagine what you might have done had you been in Bethlehem that night.

2. Remember the moment when you first believed. Share your story with your family or a friend.

3. Consider how you might "come to the manger" at some point in the holidays this year.

PRAY THIS PRAYER: *Father, thank You for saving me. Thank You for inviting me to come to the manger. Lord, let me worship You when I hold a baby, when I read stories to my children, when I bring a smile to my teenagers' face. Oh God, bring me to Your manger often this season—and give me boldness so that I might bring others to the manger too. In Jesus' precious name I pray. Amen*

CHAPTER 9

THE SHEPHERDS

*And there were shepherds living out in the fields nearby,
keeping watch over their flocks at night. An angel of the Lord
appeared to them, and the glory of the Lord shone around
them, and they were terrified!*

*But the angel said to them, "Do not be afraid. I bring you
good news of great joy that will be for all the people. Today in
the town of David a Savior has been born to you; he is Christ
the Lord. This will be a sign to you: You will find a baby
wrapped in cloths and lying in a manger."*

*Suddenly a great company of heavenly host appeared with
the angel, praising God and saying, "Glory to God in the
highest, and on earth peace to men on whom his favor rests."*

*When the angels had left them and gone into heaven,
the shepherds said to one another, "Let's go to Bethlehem
and see this thing that has happened,
which the Lord has told us about."*

*So, they hurried off and found Mary and Joseph, and the
baby, who was lying in the manger. When they had seen
him, they spread the word concerning what had been told
them about this child, and all who heard it were amazed at
what the shepherds said to them.*

Luke 2:8-18

Each figure in your nativity scene has something to teach you. They made it to Jesus' birthday party because there were characteristics in them that caused them to be more alert to the activity of God. We're going to consider each one separately in order to pinpoint these characteristics. If you'll embrace these characteristics in your own life, you will find yourself more in tune with God's work in the world today.

This is what we can know about the hearts of the shepherds: They were faithful. Their faithfulness was demonstrated in the small, lowly task of watching their sheep. They were taking good care of the sheep entrusted to them.

These shepherds were also alert. They were making sure their helpless sheep were safe, and just as they'd done hundreds of nights before—they were sleeping on the hard ground, with one eye open—ever watchful for enemies lurking in the darkness.

Here is the application: **you experience the activity of God when you are faithful and alert to the work He's given you to do.**

I know some people who are so eager to do something amazing for God that they completely miss the amazing opportunities that come in the gentle ebb and flow of daily life. Harry Jackson said this well in his book *The*

Warrior Heart: "Even if you are on an express train to fame and glory, Christian greatness lies in your attention to mundane details."

MEET ME AT THE MANGER . . .

1. What amazing things would you like to do for God?

2. How might your common life offer you opportunity to be used by God?

PRAY THIS PRAYER: *Father, don't let me be so distracted by my dreams that I miss the joy in living life. Thank You for the reminder that THIS is the day You have made. I will rejoice and be glad in it. Amen*

CHAPTER 10

POOR LOWLY SHEPHERDS

*But the angel said to them, "Do not be afraid.
I bring you good news of great joy that will be for all
the people. Today in the town of David a Savior has been
born to you; he is Christ the Lord."*
Luke 2:10-11

This was good news! For even though a Savior had been born, the shepherds might have never imagined He was actually born for them. Being a shepherd was a lowly job. Remember when David caught up with his brothers in the Valley of Elah? His brother Eliab said, "Why have you come here? And with whom did you leave those few sheep in the desert?" (1 Samuel 17:28)

Eliab was trying to humiliate David in front of the other soldiers by letting them all know that his little brother was merely a "shepherd boy." I imagine David's face turned red, and shame rose up to threaten to over-whelm him—in fact I have imagined what happened that day in my book *Women Overcoming Fear*. I love David's response to Eliab's attempt to tear him down—he simply turned away from his brother and talked to someone else (see 1 Samuel 17:30).

Isaiah 55:8-9 says, "For my thoughts are not your thoughts, neither are your ways my ways," declared the Lord. "As the heavens are higher than the earth, so are my ways higher than your ways and my thoughts than your thoughts."

Even in Jesus' day, shepherds were still considered some of the lowest class in the culture. They didn't make much money, and they weren't admired in the synagogues. They could be likened to "sanitation engineers" in our culture. Yet God, in all His wisdom, chose to invite the shepherds to His birthday party.

While we think that making a certain salary, or living in a certain house, driving a certain car or wearing a certain label might indicate "success"; I dare say there were many successful businessmen and maybe even businesswomen sleeping in the "cloud nine" beds in Bethlehem's inn. Beds they reserved far ahead of time when they knew they would be traveling there for the census—and none of them got out of bed to see the baby. No, the angels weren't sent by God to invite them to the party!

So today, we put the shepherds on our foyer tables and we remember the night they "kept their watch." And we don't give the inn-dwellers the slightest thought.

Keep your watch, and listen for the voice of God. Fulfill God's chosen plan for your life. Don't for one second think that what you are doing doesn't matter. Love those He's given you to love, keep watch over their souls by praying for them, and encouraging them, and speaking to them on His behalf. You never know when the angels might show up on one of your "watches"!

MEET ME AT THE MANGER . . .

1. How does the need to "keep up with the Joneses'" distract people from serving God?

2. Why is it harder for rich people to find the path to God?

PRAY THIS PRAYER: *Lord, while I don't consider myself rich, I am far wealthier than most of the people in the world if I'm reading this book. Thank You for my wealth. Please allow me to use my wealth to serve You; don't let my wealth keep me from trusting You. Amen*

CHAPTER 11

BE FAITHFUL IN THE SMALL THINGS

Let us not become weary in doing good, for at the proper time we will reap a harvest if we do not give up.

Galatians 6:9

The shepherds had hearts that were faithful—even in the small things. Are you faithful in the small, seemingly insignificant tasks of life?

Young mother, don't be distracted by the life you cannot lead while you are changing diapers and wiping little noses. The world would have you think that a minimum-wage-paid "worker" might do this job better than you. But, the work you do—that seems so "not spiritual"—the work of feeding, rocking, burping, and changing your babies is perhaps some of heaven's most honorable tasks.

Mother of teens—don't lose heart. They may say they don't like you just now, but deep down inside they value the security you provide in their lives. By setting firm boundaries they grow toward confident independence. Has your son or daughter rejected you? Pray for him! Pray for her! No one can pray for the wayward child like a mother can. Stay faithful to the task, keep your watch, and listen to the angels sing.

Daughters who care for your aging mothers, be encouraged! She may not even remember your name, but she loved you when you couldn't say her name either. Thank you for the dignity you allow her, and the kindness you afford her as you carefully love her in the twilight years of her life.

Wives, respect your husbands and submit to them. Scripture teaches us that when we do, we show the world how the Church respects and submits to the Lord. If your husband is not the spiritual leader of your home, pray for him. Ask the Lord to give you a quiet and gentle spirit so that the Holy Spirit might be free to work powerfully in his mind and his heart. Realize that when you do your husband's laundry you are moving mountains for the kingdom.

Don't forget that God's ways are not man's ways. The greatest work is often that which goes unnoticed by others and seems insignificant while doing it.

MEET ME AT THE MANGER . . .

1. What tasks fill your days that seem insignificant to you?

2. Would you be willing to offer these "chores" to God and trust Him with the purposes He wants to accomplish through them?

PRAY THIS PRAYER: *Father, I know that You are in the little things. You are a God of order and detail. Help me to do all my chores as if I were being watched by a stadium full of cheering fans. I know that a time will come when I will see and understand what You were doing when I was being faithful in the small things. Amen*

CHAPTER 12

TRUE GREATNESS

But the Lord said to Samuel, "Do not consider his appearance or his height, for I have rejected him. The Lord does not look at the things man looks at. Man looks at the outward appearance, but the Lord looks at the heart."

1 Samuel 16:7

I've traveled many places and met numerous people. I used to think "if only I could meet…*so and so,*" but I have met some of those "if onlys" and have often been somewhat disappointed. People that I considered "great" in the kingdom because of their fame and success have surprised me with their pretense and vanity. Not all famous Christians have disappointed me. Some of them have impressed me with their uncanny ability to deflect the attention that came their way and instead point it all toward God.

But the people who've impressed me the most are…

…the mother of a gang member on death row in California who is the only person on the face of the earth who intercedes for her son.

...the young mother with cancer who chose to give birth to her son rather than abort him to save her own life.

...the pastor of a small congregation who lived in half a single-wide trailer (the other half was where his church gathered). Why there? In that small community his congregation was the only Christian witness.

...the woman doctor who pressed through the corruption in India's government to establish a hospital for the purpose of meeting people's physical needs while ministering to their spiritual needs.

...the couple who adopted a baby girl from China—but not one who was healthy—one who had a heart defect that rushed her directly from China to ICU at Vanderbilt Hospital.

...the 73-year-old woman who told me that in October she would have celebrated her 60th wedding anniversary, only her husband died in June. With tears in her eyes she said, "no woman has been loved as well as I have been loved."

...or the pastor's wife who faithfully encourages her church-planting husband, meets the needs of her two little girls, and ministers more encouragement to countless other women (one being me).

My list could go on and on and on. These people will never have their names on fliers, websites, or bookstore displays, but they are truly great in God's kingdom—because they were faithful to live the life God called them to live, giving Him glory every step of the way.

MEET ME AT THE MANGER:

1. Read Luke 2:8-18 again and think of the shepherds' faithfulness in the lowly task of "keeping watch o're their flock by night."

2. Where are you right now in your faithfulness to the "small things" in your life?

3. Invite God to show you how He measures success.

PRAY THIS PRAYER: *Lord, forgive me for missing the joy that You offer me in the seemingly mundane activities of my days. Help me to recognize Your voice, and Your purposes in the common place and the ordinary. Today, let me do all my work as if the world were watching and the crowds were cheering. Thank You for the life You allow me to live—right here, right now. Amen*

CHAPTER 13

PA RUM PUM PUM PUM

*So they hurried off and found Mary and Joseph,
and the baby, who was lying in the manger.*

Luke 2:16

One of my favorite Christmas songs is the "Little Drummer Boy."

"The words and music to the Christmas song Little Drummer Boy was composed by Katherine K. Davis, Henry Onorati and Harry Simeone in 1958. ...Little Drummer Boy has been a huge hit for several artists. The most notable rendition was created by the most unlikely combination of Bing Crosby and David Bowie. This version of Little Drummer Boy was a massive hit for the artists and was in fact Bing Crosby's most successful recording since the legendary White Christmas."

(www.carols.org.uk/little_drummer_boy)

The song is about a little shepherd boy who doesn't want to go see the baby Jesus without a gift. Finally he decides that he can give the baby a song, and he plays his little drum.

LITTLE DRUMMER BOY: LYRICS

Come they told me, pa rum pum pum pum
A new born King to see, pa rum pum pum pum
Our finest gifts we bring, pa rum pum pum pum
To lay before the King, pa rum pum pum pum,
rum pum pum pum, rum pum pum pum,

So to honor Him, pa rum pum pum pum,
When we come.

Little Baby, pa rum pum pum pum
I am a poor boy too, pa rum pum pum pum
I have no gift to bring, pa rum pum pum pum
That's fit to give the King, pa rum pum pum pum,
rum pum pum pum, rum pum pum pum,

Shall I play for you, pa rum pum pum pum,
On my drum?

Mary nodded, pa rum pum pum pum
The ox and lamb kept time, pa rum pum pum pum
I played my drum for Him, pa rum pum pum pum
I played my best for Him, pa rum pum pum pum,
rum pum pum pum, rum pum pum pum,

Then He smiled at me, pa rum pum pum pum
Me and my drum.

Besides having an easy melody, and plenty of pa rum pum pum pums, I love the story. Can't you see the little boy carefully playing his little drum for the tiny baby?

Meet me at the manger . . .

1. I would imagine that the tradition of gift giving most likely goes on during your family's Christmas celebration. What makes Christmas gifts special?

2. Have you considered what you might give Jesus?

Pray this prayer: *Father, I know that You don't desire burnt offerings and sacrifices—You're also not interested in the pretty trinkets we wrap with foil and ribbons. You want me to offer myself to You with no strings attached. You've given me so much—to give myself to You is the least that I can do. Thank You for wanting me! Amen*

CHAPTER 14

GIFT GIVING

For we are God's workmanship,
created in Christ Jesus to do good works,
which God prepared in advance for us to do.
Ephesians 2:10

My daughter Mikel loves to give gifts. It must be one of her love languages. She had her first boyfriend when she was 15, and during their six-week relationship, she gave him a hat, a pocket knife, a CD or two, and I can't remember what else. Every Christmas we discuss the possibility of *not* giving gifts to one another. We struggle with the "too much money spent on too many things" that competes with the real meaning of Christmas. But when we threaten to shut the gift-giving down (or at least keep it to a minimum) Mikel has a fit. She cannot imagine celebrating Christmas without giving gifts. Last year she talked me into letting her be Santa for my parents (her grandparents) and my sisters (her aunts). We got up before the sun did on Christmas morning and laid out the carefully chosen gifts to surprise them with Santa's visit. I think that Mikel was more excited about that surprise than she was about anything she opened for herself that day.

She's a junior in high school today. And she is thinking about what she might want to do vocationally with her life. I'm teaching her (and my other two children) that if they are serious about giving their lives to Christ, then they don't have to figure out what they want to do with their lives…instead they have to figure out what God wants to do with their lives. I tell them that God had "good works prepared in advance." And that He thought, "Hmm, I wonder who might contribute to that work? Oh, I could form Mikel to complete that particular task." Then, He initiated the miracle of her conception.

For we are God's workmanship, created in Christ Jesus to do good works, which God prepared in advance for us to do. (Ephesians 2:10)

This is more than great advice for teenagers seeking direction for their lives. Realizing that our lives are not our own—and acting on that realization is worship. Tom said this morning in his sermon that true worship focuses on a Person (the Person of Jesus Christ), and that when we worship in spirit and truth, we are much more interested in what we offer to God than we are in what we are getting from the experience. (He mentioned the spiritual goose bumps we love and often feel when we sing and offer our praise.) He said this with a whole lot more enthusiasm, and a bit of jiggle in his hips—and I have a hard time relaying his message on paper the way he delivered it in person. But the truth remains.

We respond to God's love by offering Him our worship. We worship the Lord when we give Him the gift of our lives.

Therefore, I urge you, brothers, in view of God's mercy, to offer your bodies as living sacrifices, holy and pleasing to God—this is your spiritual act of worship. (Romans 12:1-2)

Meet me at the Manger . . .

1. How might you serve God with your gifts, talents, and time?

2. Who has God put in your life that He wants you to serve?

Pray this prayer: *Lord, when I realize that You had "good work" in mind for me before You made me, I am eager to understand exactly what that work involves. I don't want to waste my minutes doing things that were not created for me to do. I want my life to matter—I want to fulfill the good work You prepared in advance for me to do. Amen*

CHAPTER 15

I'LL PLAY MY DRUM FOR HIM

*For God so loved the world that He gave
His only begotten Son, that whoever believes in Him,
should not perish but have eternal life.*
John 3:16 NASB

The little drummer boy was on to something when he played that drum. He offered his gifts and his talents, his time, and his energy. He expressed his adoration and his love by beating on his drum. What has God given you that you can play for Him?

Part of my role as a mother is to help my children identify their unique package of gifts, talents, interests, and personality. Mikel has compassion, love for children, a competitive spirit, and tenacity. Kaleigh has a heart for the poor; she's a terrific problem-solver and is almost fluent in Spanish. TJ is fair, generous, and has never met someone who couldn't be his friend. Tom is a great leader, a gifted speaker, competitive, and full of perseverance. Me? I'm a writer. I love to teach, and I'm sentimental almost to a fault. Why do I share this with you? Not because I want to brag on my family members—but rather to help you understand the connection that exists between our lives and *the good work God prepared in advance* for us to do. All of these talents and characteristics are indicators of what God had in mind when He created us. They are God's hints to help us discover the "good work."

At this point in time my children are still working out the details of God's plan for their lives. But Mikel plans to pursue a degree in elementary education. Kaleigh plans to be a doctor. And TJ—TJ wants to have as many friends as possible as he continues to navigate his way through high school. My husband Tom is a pastor—and I'm a writer and speaker. We've already prayed through God's plans for our lives and are living them out.

In the holiday season when we want to wrap our love in a box and tie it with a bow, God is asking you to give Him something much more valuable than that. He gave His best for you.

For God so loved the world that He gave His only begotten Son… (John 3:16)

What can you give to Him?

Our finest gifts we bring, pa rum pum pum pum
To lay before the King, pa rum pum pum pum,
rum pum pum pum, rum pum pum pum,

So to honor Him, pa rum pum pum pum,
When we come.

MEET ME AT THE MANGER . . .

1. Underline Romans 12:1-2 in your copy of God's Word.

2. The little drummer boy had a drum. What do you have that you can use to give a gift to God?

PRAY THIS PRAYER: *Father, You have given me so much. Life, family, a home, [be specific…]. Thank You for giving the best gift of all when You sent Your very own Son to die for my sins. I want to offer You the gift of me this holiday season. I give You my life. Amen*

CHAPTER 16

THE WISE MEN

*After Jesus was born in Bethlehem of Judea in the days of
King Herod, wise men from the east arrived unexpectedly
in Jerusalem, saying, "Where is He who has been
born King of the Jews? For we saw His star in the east and
have come to worship Him."*
Matthew 2:1-2 HCSB

"Three wise women would have asked direc-
tions, arrived on time, helped deliver the baby,
cleaned the stable, made a casserole, brought
practical gifts, and there would be peace on earth"
(Anonymous, read on a holiday towel found in a small
mountain shop).

Don't you know it? But, our nativity scenes don't
include three wise women. Matthew's gospel records the
visit of the wise men. And, aren't we glad he did? They
simply add class to our nativity scenes (not to mention an
international flavor).

*After Jesus was born in Bethlehem in Judea, during the
time of King Herod, Magi from the east came to Jerusalem
and asked, "Where is the one who has been born king of the
Jews? We saw his star in the east and have come to worship
him."*

When King Herod heard this he was disturbed, and all Jerusalem with him. [note: King Herod was somewhat disturbed when the wise men were not in town; and most often his disturbances meant death or suffering for others. That is why, I imagine, that all Jerusalem was disturbed with him.] *When he had called together all the peoples' chief priests and teachers of the law, he asked them where the Christ was to be born. "In Bethlehem in Judea," they replied. "for this is what the prophet has written:*

But you, Bethlehem, in the land of Judah, are by no means least among the rulers of Judah; for out of you will come a ruler who will be the shepherd of my people Israel.

Then Herod called the Magi secretly and found out from them the exact time the star had appeared. He sent them to Bethlehem and said, "Go and make a careful search for the child. As soon as you find him, report to me, so that I too may go and worship him."

After they had heard the king, they went on their way, and the star they had seen in the east went ahead of them until it stopped over the place where the child was. When they saw the star, they were overjoyed. On coming to the house, they saw the child with his mother, Mary, and they bowed down and worshipped him. Then they opened their treasures and presented him with gifts of gold and of incense and of myrrh. And having been warned in a dream not to go back to Herod, they returned to their country by another route. (Matthew 2:1-12)

MEET ME AT THE MANGER . . .

1. Although we put our wise men near the manger they most likely arrived long after Joseph and Mary vacated the barn. Can you imagine what they might have talked about as they traveled?

2. Have you ever searched for something long and hard—then been excited to find it? What did it feel like to be searching? How did you feel when you found what you were looking for?

PRAY THIS PRAYER: *Lord, I want to be wise like these men. I want to set my eyes on You and steer a steady path toward Your destiny for my life. Help me when I grow discouraged and give me perseverance to stay the course. I know that what You have for me is better than anything else. Amen*

CHAPTER 17

MAGI FROM THE EAST

Then Herod secretly summoned the wise men and asked
them the exact time the star appeared.
Matthew 2:7 HCSB

Magi they are called. We know they came from the east and that they brought at least three gifts. Traditionally we've believed there were three of them, and that they traveled for days to see the baby Jesus. I wonder what they'd read to cause them to believe that a king had been born? There is a traditional belief in China that Liu Shang—the chief astrologer in the Han Dynasty—discovered the "king star" (a star that shone every time a king was born), and that he disappeared two years after the star appeared suggesting that he might have been one of the men making the trip.

When the wise men arrived in Bethlehem they went to the obvious place to find a baby king; they went to the palace. And that is when King Herod discovered the birth of Jesus. Imagine that. The most amazing birth that ever happened took place right in his own backyard and Herod (the most powerful man in the vicinity) didn't know a thing about it. He hadn't heard of the angels singing (although the shepherds no doubt spread that story far and wide). He totally missed the light of the star. And, he was oblivious to the prophecies that indicated that Bethlehem would be Jesus' birthplace.

In contrast to King Herod who ate, drank, and slept in Bethlehem but completely missed Jesus—the wise men traveled from far away because they were convinced He was worth the effort. They brought gifts to present to him and intended to worship this amazing boy. The wise men were wise because they studied. They had hearts that were seeking. The men who traveled "from afar" spent their days studying the writings of old, and their nights studying the heavens. They kept their eyes and their minds open—and they searched for truth. Because they were looking—because they were seeking—they saw what others missed. The wise men saw a star, and out of wonder, mystery, and in great hope they followed that star all the way to Bethlehem.

Here is the application: **When we study God's Word, and search for His truth—we will discover wonder and joy and peace and power that others might completely miss.**

Can you imagine how these men must have felt when they found the Christ child? They'd left home and spent many nights sleeping outside; fighting bandits perhaps; eating hard bread and cheese...when finally they came to a house where a simple carpenter and a young mother lived with their baby boy.

Their studies indicated that a great king had been born. Most likely they charted the moment the star first appeared, and the time it took them to make their journey. While they didn't know the exact location of this newborn king, they did know his approximate age. So when Herod knew nothing of the birth of Jesus, they most likely asked around. "Who knows of a family with a young boy, say around two years old?" And finally when the home matched the coordinates of the star, they knocked on the door. (I'm glad Mary was faithful in the small things—and that she was home with Jesus rather than off working, having left Him in the care of a friend.)

MEET ME AT THE MANGER . . .

1. Have you developed the discipline of reading God's Word on a daily basis? If not, start doing that today!

2. A genuine search for truth accompanied with diligent effort toward living the truth will give your life stability and joy. Do you *know* this to be true?

PRAY THIS PRAYER: *Father, I know that Jesus said the truth would make me free. There is so much deception in my world. I need Your Truth. Help me to discipline myself to be in Your Word on a daily basis so that I will fill my mind with TRUTH every single day. Strengthen me also to take captive each and every thought and make it bow down to the lordship of Christ. Amen*

CHAPTER 18

WHAT MADE
THE WISE MEN WISE?

*Entering the house, they saw the child with Mary His
mother, and falling on their knees, they worshiped Him.
Then they opened their treasures and presented Him with
gifts: gold, frankincense, and myrrh.*

Matthew 2:11 HCSB

You know how I know these men were wise? Scripture says that when they found Jesus in a common house with a common mother (as opposed to being in a palace with a governess) they "fell on their knees and worshiped Him" then they opened their treasures and presented them to Him. While others might have insisted that the King of the Jews be somehow related to Herod, the wise men understood that God's ways are higher than man's. They didn't limit truth by making it squeeze in traditional boxes.

The wise men thought beyond the parameters of this world. They could have been disappointed and considered their trip a flop when King Herod knew nothing about the baby. They could have wondered if they'd followed the wrong star or taken a wrong turn or misinterpreted the ancient writings. But instead, they stayed the course, and allowed God to reveal Jesus to them—outside the trappings of an earthly king's castle.

It might have been easy for the wise men to declare: "Well this isn't a king at all! He's just a little boy—the simple son of a carpenter!" They could have saved their gifts to give to Herod when they retraced their steps on their return trip home. But instead, they believed (and saw) Jesus as He truly was...the mighty King of kings and Lord of lords. And they gave their gifts (fit for a king) to this simple little boy. Many scholars believe the gold is what funded Joseph and Mary's escape to Egypt following their visit from the wise men.

Consider why, even to this day, we continue to call these men "wise." The wise men had wise hearts that allowed God to show them mysteries that were hidden to the supposedly "wise men" (and rulers) of this world.

1 Corinthians 1:27 says, "But God chose the foolish things of the world to shame the wise; God chose the weak things of the world to shame the strong."

It is just like God to take ordinary people like you and me—and draw us into the mystery of His love! If we will allow Him, God will open our minds and hearts to understand truths that others might completely miss. And when we understand truth, we will be able to contribute to God's work!

Notice also the practicality of their gifts. The wise men most likely funded Joseph, Mary, and Jesus' escape to Egypt—God used "wise men" then just like He uses wise men and women today to partner with Him in funding and accomplishing His kingdom purposes.

Oh Lord, use us today—to impact Your world—give us a deep hunger to seek TRUTH and walk in it.

MEET ME AT THE MANGER . . .

1. Read the rest of the story in Matthew 2:13-23. Notice the violence that accompanied Jesus' birth. See the spiritual warfare—and the provision of God.

2. How can you be wise?

PRAY THIS PRAYER: *Father, I want to be wise. Give me a hunger and thirst for Your Word. When others look around, keep me looking up. And, help me to trust You when You lead me to places I've never been before. Help me to think beyond the boundaries, to dream big dreams and believe. In Jesus' name I pray. Amen*

CHAPTER 19

WHERE ARE THE WISE MEN TODAY?

At Gibeon the Lord appeared to Solomon during the night in a dream, and God said, "Ask for whatever you want me to give you." Solomon answered, "You have shown kindness to your servant, my father David, because he was faithful to you and righteous and upright in heart. You have continued this great kindness to him and have given him a son to sit on his throne this very day. Now, O Lord my God, you have made your servant king in place of my father David. But I am only a little child and do not know how to carry out my duties. Your servant is here among the people you have chosen, a great people, too numerous to count or number. So give your servant a discerning heart to govern your people and to distinguish between right and wrong.

For who is able to govern this great people of yours?"

I Kings 3:5-9

Solomon was the wisest of men because God was pleased that when he could have asked for anything, he asked for wisdom. Of course Solomon was also the richest and most honored among men as well because God saw fit to give him more than what he requested. God strongly supports wise men (and women).

I was sitting in a conference in Washington, DC, listening to some of our most powerful Christian statesmen tell us how we might better influence our nation for God when my mind wandered back to these wise men who worshipped Jesus. I came up with four things that characterize wise men:

1. Wise men journey toward Jesus. Even if their journey takes them far from home, costs them greatly, and takes unexpected twists and turns, wise men don't stop until they find Him.

2. Wise men worship Jesus. Even if He doesn't look like they think He should look—and even if they find themselves worshiping on the dirt floor of a carpenter's house rather than the marble floor of a palace.

3. Wise men give generously to Jesus. I'm not sure what a baby needed with gold, frankincense, and myrrh—but that didn't matter to the wise men. He was a king worthy of sacrifice.

4. Wise men use their wealth and their influence to advance the causes of God. The wise men never went back to Herod because they were warned in a dream not to. What might have happened if the wise men had refused to give their gifts to Jesus and instead gone back to Herod to tell him what they'd discovered?

Where are the wise men (and wise women) today?

MEET ME AT THE MANGER . . .

1. What do you do to journey toward Jesus? How tenacious are you about finding Him?

2. How do you worship Jesus? Do you kneel before Him in the wonder of His majesty?

3. Do you give generously to Jesus? What kind of sacrifice have you made to Him?

4. Which of God's kingdom plans might be released today with your generosity of wealth and influence?

PRAY THIS PRAYER: *Lord, make me a wise man/woman today. Amen*

CHAPTER 20

WISDOM IS SUPREME

Wisdom is supreme; therefore get wisdom.
Though it cost all you have, get understanding.
Esteem her, and she will honor you. She will set
a garland of grace on your head and present you
with a crown of splendor.

Proverbs 4:7-9

This Scripture is one of Solomon's proverbs. He had wisdom and knew it was more valuable than anything else.

Watch how the world celebrates Christmas. If you're not careful, you will be subtly drawn into its deception. The deceptive nature of our enemy is what makes wisdom critical in our lives. See how the prince of this world uses Santa Claus to lure God's children away from the manger.

Do you know the true legend of jolly old Saint Nicholas? Legend has it that a wealthy man secretly dropped gold coins in the stockings of poor girls when the stockings hung by the fire at night to dry. The coins were collected as a dowry so the girls could afford to be married. In Saint Nicholas' day, women without husbands were poverty-stricken, with no hope of a future. This benevolent man didn't want to be honored for his generosity, so he secretly hid the coins.

How did we go from that thoughtful deed to the bearded man, dressed in a red suit sitting in our shopping malls today? Today's Santa is intent on breeding greed into the hearts and minds of our children. "What do you want for Christmas?" With that simple question the unspoken assumption is that there is something they lack. (Sounds a little bit like Satan's first interaction with Eve in the garden.) Cleverly the focus at Christmas is stolen from a celebration of gratitude and worship of what we already have—and instead placed on the one or two things the advertisers have convinced us we need.

Consider television commercials year-round. They don't sell beer—they sell friendship and good times. They don't sell jewelry or perfume—they sell love and seduction. Why, if it is a car you are buying, does it have to come with a beautiful woman or the backwoods or adventure? The list could go on and on. Even those marketing their wares during the Christmas season understand that we don't need more "stuff." With their marketing schemes, they try to convince us that the "stuff" they want to sell will give us what we really desire (the deeper things of the heart).

We celebrate this time of the year not for what we have yet to receive but for what God has already given. Why is it so hard for us to understand that the Christ child IS the present? The wise men knew He was. They brought gifts to Him—while we sit back and beg Him to bring gifts to us.

MEET ME AT THE MANGER . . .

1. Do you practice the tradition of Santa in your home? If so, how can you make sure to keep the spotlight on Jesus?

2. "Santa" came to visit my children. I'm not sure he did them any harm. The best way we've taught our children to be grateful is by sending them on mission trips to third-world countries. How will you teach your children to develop an attitude of gratitude?

PRAY THIS PRAYER: *Oh God, thank You for opening my eyes to the many ways the enemy tricks us into missing You each Christmas. Let me be the one in my family to insist that You remain the center of our holiday celebration. You alone are deserving of the attention. Amen*

CHAPTER 21

JOLLY OLD SAINT NICHOLAS

Delight yourself in the Lord,
and He will give you the desires of your heart.
Psalm 37:4

Santa Claus does great harm to the concept of prayer. Many Christians treat God like children treat Santa. They bring their list of "stuff," climb up in his lap—invite Him to "lean His ear this way"—then jump down and do their best to "be good, not bad" so that He'll deliver what they've requested.

That reminds me of the song my mother sang in hopes of keeping us tolerable during the days leading up to Christmas:

"You better watch out, you better not cry, you better not pout I'm telling you why…Santa Claus is coming to town. He's making a list, checking it twice, gonna find out who's naughty and nice…Santa Claus is coming to town. He knows when you are sleeping. He knows when you're awake. He knows if you've been bad or good so be good for goodness sake. You better watch out, you better not cry, you better not pout I'm telling you why…Santa Claus is coming to town!"

Some people still believe in Santa Claus. They still believe that if they give God their list, then try their best not to pout and cry, God is obligated to fulfill their desires. I used to think this way myself. I thought that as long as I did my part to live up to the standard of God's Word—you know, "don't cheat, don't smoke, don't drink, don't chew, and don't go with boys who do"—then God would give me my heart's desire. In fact, there is a verse in Psalm 37:4,

"Delight yourself in the Lord, and He will give you the desires of your heart."

I used to think that this verse was a promise for prosperity. (Prosperity being whatever I chose for it to be at that moment in my life.) If only I would trust God to give me that list, then He would!! If only I would muster up my faith—and choose to believe God would shower His favor on me! But that was before I watched mothers, children, fathers, and other really amazing people die; deal with severe handicaps; suffer debilitating diseases; and endure the loss of jobs. These were not heathens that I watched walk those paths. They were good, God-fearing, God-honoring children of the faith.

MEET ME AT THE MANGER . . .

1. How has Santa Claus Imparted your prayer life?

2. What happens to your faith when bad things happen to good people?

3. Read John 16:33.

PRAY THIS PRAYER: *Oh God—how much the world has penetrated my faith. Please forgive me for thinking that I can manipulate You to give me what I want when I want it. Forgive me for treating You like Santa Claus. I know that You are the Lord of lords and King of kings. I know that I will be much better off receiving what You want me to have over and above getting what I think I want from You. Amen*

CHAPTER 22

THE PRESENCE OF GOD

*You have made known to me the path of life;
you will fill me with joy in your presence,
with eternal pleasures at your right hand.*

Psalm 16:11

What did the wise men know that many of us don't? They knew that riches were made to be given away—and that stars lit by God were worthy of following. When they worshipped the Christ child, they knew that to "delight yourself in the Lord" meant to find your greatest treasures in the presence of God. If the wise men who visited Jesus were familiar with the Psalms, they might have prayed,

You have made known to me the path of life; you will fill me with joy in your presence, with eternal pleasures at your right hand. (Psalm 16:11)

Most likely they already knew what took me several years to discover—the true meaning of Psalm 37:4. The first part of that verse says,

Delight yourself in the Lord.

This means that you find your joy in His presence. Find your satisfaction in Him. Grow to understand how He alone fulfills your craving. Realize that nothing you can buy, wrap, decorate, and place under your tree can even begin to compare with Him. Unlike the Santas in the mall—you don't have to jump up after your picture's been taken and your list delivered. The time in His lap IS your gift. And the price tag was high.

The second part of Psalm 37:4 promises that,

…He will give you the desires of your heart.

When you sit in the lap of God, and find your delight in Him—He will put into your heart, and He will take out of your heart what He wants you to desire. He will create His desires in you. The wise men were impacted by the heart of God. Because they were hungry for truth, God gave them the desire to take the journey to Bethlehem. And in the end, their hunger was satisfied when they bowed before the Truth of God (in the person of His Son).

Wisdom is supreme; therefore get wisdom. Though it cost all you have, get understanding. Esteem her, and she will exalt you; embrace her, and she will honor you. She will set a garland of grace on your head and present you with a crown of splendor. (Proverbs 4:7-9)

MEET ME AT THE MANGER . . .

1. Why is wisdom so important?

2. What do you need to commit to the Lord? What desires of your heart do you long for Him to have sovereignty over?

PRAY THIS PRAYER: *Father, I want Christmas to be a time of joy and special memories. I want my children to learn the significance of this holiday—and to ponder the things of life that really matter. Help me to be intentional about teaching them as I choose which traditions to embrace—and which to reject. I commit my heart to You and yield it to Your desires. In Jesus name I pray. Amen*

CHAPTER 23

JOSEPH

This is how the birth of Jesus Christ came about: His mother Mary was pledged to be married to Joseph, but before they came together, she was found to be with child through the Holy Spirit. Because Joseph her husband was a righteous man and did not want to expose her to public disgrace, he had in mind to divorce her quietly.

But after he had considered this, an angel of the Lord appeared to Him in a dream and said, "Joseph son of David, do not be afraid to take Mary home as your wife, because what is conceived in her is from the Holy Spirit. She will give birth to a son, and you are to give him the name Jesus, because he will save his people from their sins."

All this took place to fulfill what the Lord had said through the prophet: "The virgin will be with child and will give birth to a son, and they will call Him Immanuel"—which means, "God with us."

When Joseph woke up, he did what the angel of the Lord had commanded him and took Mary home as his wife.

But he had no union with her until she gave birth to a son. And he gave him the name Jesus.

Matthew 1:18-25

There are several phrases in this passage of Scripture that amaze me. The first is this: "...but before they came together, she was found to be with child through the Holy Spirit."

Now, because we sit on this side of Jesus' birth, earthly ministry, death, and resurrection, we say, "of course Mary was pregnant by the Holy Spirit!" We consider Jesus' conception "immaculate." And, we call Mary "blessed." But, had we lived down the street from Mary—and had she been "found to be with child"—we would have surmised that she'd either been with Joseph in a way that was not proper—or worse, that she had been with another man besides Joseph although she was pledged to Joseph. In her day, Mary's pregnancy would have been considered a crisis. Don't forget that.

Just imagine Mary whispering to you, "I'm pregnant—but the father of my child is the Holy Spirit!"

Right... In fact, that's exactly how Joseph felt.

MEET ME AT THE MANGER . . .

1. We don't pause slowly enough to digest the wonder of the Christmas story. Take three minutes right now to pretend you are either Mary or Joseph and you are dealing with the reality of this unusual pregnancy. What are you thinking? How do you feel?

2. Has God ever asked you to do something that others misunderstood? Who did He place in your life to encourage you?

PRAY THIS PRAYER: *Father, thank You for taking care of Mary. Thank You for Joseph. I would love to sit and chat with him someday. To think of how he jumped in the gossip mill with Mary and endured the suspicions of all their friends and neighbors. Thank You for taking care of them every step of the way. Help me to be bold when/if You ask me to do something for You that might make others think less of me. Amen*

CHAPTER 24

JOSEPH WAS A RIGHTEOUS MAN

*…Because Joseph her husband was a righteous man
and did not want to expose her to public disgrace,
he had in mind to divorce her quietly.*

Matthew 1:19

This phrase also amazes me. In order to understand why, you need to read John 8:1-11. This is the account of Jesus' encounter with the woman caught in (the very act of) adultery. Scripture records that the "teachers of the law and the Pharisees brought" this woman to Jesus. They flung her before him in the courtyard of the synagogue and demanded that Jesus tell them what to do with her. These *self-righteous* men publicly disgraced this woman.

I find it interesting that Matthew calls Joseph "righteous" because he *didn't* want Mary to be publicly disgraced. Isn't that interesting? The Pharisees and teachers of the law defined righteousness for the people and yet acted in a way that even their own society might deem unkind.

Nevertheless, Joseph was a righteous man. He was also a compassionate man. His righteousness dictated that he must not carry through with his plans to marry her—but his compassion determined to divorce her quietly. This was Joseph's way of "figuring out" his problem with Mary.

The third phrase that amazes me is the one that tells about another encounter with an angel. This time, it happened in a dream:

"But after he had considered this, an angel of the Lord appeared to him in a dream and said, 'Joseph son of David, do not be afraid to take Mary home as your wife, because what is conceived in her is from the Holy Spirit.'"

Isn't that great? Mary couldn't convince Joseph that she was telling him the truth, so God sent an angel to intervene. Not only that, but the angel told Joseph that he was also a critical partner in Jesus' birth as well. For the angel assumed that Joseph would take Mary to be his wife, protect her from the rumors and slander, and give her both a home and a name. Not only that, Joseph would also be the one to name God's Son, Jesus.

Joseph believed. His dream powerfully impacted both his heart and his head, for rather than carry out his original plan, instead Joseph acted on what was said to him by the angel. Joseph took Mary to be his wife, and he allowed her to remain a virgin until Jesus was born.

Joseph offers us a great example of how to navigate our way through life's surprises. As men and women of

God we should calmly "consider" what to do (see Matthew 1:20) and then wait for God to confirm it. Sometimes our initial reaction is wrong. If we are careful to command our emotions to rest a bit, God will lead us through the confusion.

MEET ME AT THE MANGER . . .

1. I'm not sure I know a man today that would do what Joseph did. He allowed his reputation to be stained by Mary's pregnancy. He gave up his marriage bed. He protected and cared for Mary—even to the point of assisting in the delivery of Jesus. How would you describe Joseph?

2. What qualities did Joseph have that made him a man God could use?

PRAY THIS PRAYER: *Father, thank You for including the story from Joseph's perspective. It makes the situation more real in my mind. Following You is dangerous! And many times friends and family will be confused by my obedience. But help me to be like Joseph and follow anyway. Amen*

CHAPTER 25

LIFE IS FULL OF SURPRISES

So do not fear, for I am with you; do not be dismayed,
for I am your God. I will strengthen you and help you;
I will uphold you with my righteous right hand.

Isaiah 41:10

Here are some other things we know about Joseph by reading what Scripture says about his role in Jesus' birth and childhood. Joseph was a humble man. In his culture the firstborn son was an extension of the father. He carried the family name and the family blessing. Joseph completely yielded his "right" as a father of a firstborn son to the Lord. Joseph was a protector—he fled to Egypt with Mary and Jesus to save Him from Herod. Joseph was a provider—he worked as a carpenter to support his family.

Here is the application: **When you choose to believe, and to live out what you believe even when life surprises you, you will experience the amazing grace and love of God on all sides.**

Life is full of surprises! Sons and daughters get divorced; teens get pregnant outside of marriage; cancer is no respecter of persons; even Christian families deal up close and personal with homosexuality, depression, and suicide. Any of these things could turn your world upside down and some do. Can you imagine how Joseph's world was turned upside down when he discovered Mary was pregnant? I can just about hear him talking with a trusted friend:

"I trusted her! What has she done?! Who could it be?"

"Maybe she was forced—perhaps it was Simeon. I've seen how he looks at her when you're not around." Joseph's friend might have responded.

"She said it was the Holy Spirit."

"You gotta be kidding me!" Joseph's friend probably had to restrain himself from laughing out loud.

"No, I wish I were! What would make her make up such a story? She's frightened, that's all—she's scared out of her mind. I can't have her exposed; I won't do it."

"She deserves it, you know. And no one would think less of you. Mary must not be what you thought she was—better you find out now than later." Joseph's friend might have solemnly suggested that he go ahead and present her to the Pharisees for judgment.

"I won't. I will not do that to her. And if you say a word of this to another you'll wish you'd never been born." Joseph was more than capable of making good on that promise and his friend knew it.

This conversation most likely never took place, but it could have. Joseph was devastated by Mary's pregnancy. But instead of sorting it out alone, he listened to the voice of God.

No matter what life throws your way, when you cling to the Lord, you will find that He holds you with a grip much firmer than one with which you can hold Him. When you trust Him you will find that He is trustworthy. And if you would be so bold as to be open to be used by Him in each and every one of the crises that come your way, you will play a key role in fulfilling God's purposes in your own life and in the lives of those you consider dear.

Perhaps the greatest thing about Joseph's heart was that He was willing—willing to serve his part in God's redemption plan.

Meet me at the manger . . .

1. What amazes you most about Joseph?

2. What surprises has life tossed your way this year?

3. How might you partner with God in those circumstances?

4. The angel told Joseph what God was up to in his life, and in Mary's life. What is God up to in your life? What is God's Word to you?

PRAY THIS PRAYER: *Father, when the rug is pulled out from under me, protect me from making decisions that distance me from Your purpose in my life. Open my eyes, my ears, and my heart to understand what You are up to—and to trust You so that I can participate with You in the lives of those I love. Amen*

CHAPTER 26

EMBRACING LIFE!

…he had in mind to divorce her quietly…
Matthew 1:19

As I thought about how Joseph might have felt when he first discovered Mary's pregnancy I was reminded of this lesson I wrote in my book *Women Embracing Life…All of It!* The book challenges us to discern God's activity in our lives when circumstances catch us off guard. I use my first experience with snow skiing as an illustration for the truths I discovered in God's Word. This devotion tells of a day that I (unlike Joseph) chose poorly.

Ski trails not only have colors to distinguish them, but they also have names. The names supposedly predict the experience one might expect on that particular trail (Sheer Rocko, Tango, Freeway—to name a few). The gentler trails are designated by the color green (which is definitely for "go" not stop), and they have gentler names. Tom talked me and our three children into going with him to the top of the mountain, which happened to be the continental divide. Once we were up there we could follow the green trails down the mountain. Here's how that journey went for me:

Finally we left "Sky Walker" behind, and I actually survived Sleepy Hollow. But somewhere on Tenderfoot I came unglued.

This is not the way Tom tells the story, and it's not what he thinks happened, but this is my story, and I know exactly how it happened.

I'd had it. My nerves were frazzled. Yes, my children were fine; somehow the mercy and grace of God extends further than our good sense and He safely tucked Mikel, Kaleigh, and TJ into the protective cover of His wing. They were doing well; only a few times did they build up speed that somewhat intimidated them. I, on the other hand, had suffered visions of crumpled children and broken futures all the way down a mountain I never even wanted to go up.

I had just gained an ounce of confidence on my bunny slope only to lose it with the first experience of wind in my face as I perched precariously on the continental divide. My good husband, who happens to be great at every sport he's ever attempted, had pushed me past my limit. I wanted so much to be a cool mom, but this was ridiculous. With my skis sailing me much faster than I cared to sail, I spotted my "out"—my only hope on an otherwise hopeless trail of terror.

I didn't want to fall down so I aimed my two slick sticks of wood toward a tree. It wasn't a huge tree, nor was it small. I calculated that it was just big enough to stop me without crushing the life out of me.

No, Tom, I didn't *accidentally* hit a tree.

I purposely aimed my skis just so they would straddle the trunk of that tree. If snow plowing could slow one down, surely hitting a tree could stop one.

And hit the tree I did.

MEET ME AT THE MANGER . . .

1. What do you turn to when life gets difficult?

2. Do the things of this world satisfy you in the crunch?

PRAY THIS PRAYER: *Father I know that the things of this world will never really satisfy me. When life doesn't go my way, help me to nestle close to You so that I don't resort to crashing into trees. Amen*

CHAPTER 27

CONSIDER YOUR OPTIONS

But after he had considered this, an angel of the Lord
appeared to him in a dream and said, "Joseph son of David,
do not be afraid to take Mary home as your wife, because
what is conceived in her is from the Holy Spirit."
Matthew 1:20

Yesterday's devotion was about my crashing into a tree (on purpose). Have you ever been there? Pressed far beyond your sanity and way past your ability with too many things that are important to you left to fend for themselves—you finally give up. But noticing that it's not exactly the time or the place to "stop the train so I can get off," you create your own escape route.

Mine was a tree. What's yours? (Joseph's was going to be a quiet divorce.) What do you bang into when you've had enough of God and His pressing you past your limits? Alcohol? Chocolate? Romance novels? Prescription drugs? Sex? Divorce? Rebellion?

The more serious choices carry harsher offenses toward those you love; the more innocent ones risk being overlooked as "soft" sin and therefore never confessed. But I want you to know today that if you are serious about following hard after Christ, then you must see your "tree" for what it is—a volitional decision to step away from the purposes and plans of God. The things you rush toward in order to get off the path of God are as detrimental to God's activity in your life as my tree was to me.

Oh friends, it's time to turn loose of our trees and trust in our Savior.

He hung on one so that we wouldn't have to.

Joseph was wise enough not to react quickly to Mary's pregnancy. Scripture doesn't tell us how long he considered his options, but we do know that he slept on it. For it was while Joseph was sleeping that the angel spoke to him in a dream.

Life is full of all kinds of surprises; some of them are good, and some of them are not. When you are caught off guard and think you have nowhere to turn, be careful not to act too quickly. Most often our quick reactions are driven more by emotion than by reason. Do what Joseph did and give God time to speak clearly to you in a dream.

MEET ME AT THE MANGER . . .

1. How have you stepped away from God in difficult times? How have you pressed closer to Him?

2. How has God led you when you took the time to wait and hear His voice?

PRAY THIS PRAYER: *Lord, I know that disaster will come my way. When it does I want to turn to You. Please show me the things I've chosen to run to instead of You. I confess that turning to these things is like worshipping a "lesser god." I want to worship You only. You alone are worthy. Amen*

CHAPTER 28

GOD IS HERE

When Joseph woke up, he did what the angel of the Lord had commanded him and took Mary home as his wife.
Matthew 1:24

It had to take a whole lot of courage for Joseph to take Mary to be his wife. But in each of our lives there will come a day when God invites us to set aside our own solutions to our problems and trust Him with His.

There's more to my story from two days ago. I'm still quoting from my book *Women Embracing Life…All of it!*

Tom couldn't believe it, "Leighann, honey, are you alright?" He side-stepped with his skis up the hill to where I was clinging to my evergreen rescue. I loved that tree. Even if it did knock the wind out of me; I seriously *loved* that tree! Secretly adoring my tree, I was not secretly adoring my husband!

"Of course I'm not alright! You can't hit a tree going 50 mph and be okay! You can't put me on top of a mountain with my three children, not knowing how they can ski, set me downhill and expect me to be okay! I can't ski, they are in a dangerous place, I can't do this…"

…at which time I melted and poured forth tears.

Husbands hate it when we melt, but sometimes it can't be helped. This was definitely one of those times! And even though crying may not change the circumstances, those tears somehow lube the pain and really do help me feel better.

"Where are you hurt?" Tom's concern was showing on his face.

I was still holding tight to my tree when I (not too nicely) replied, "I don't know, but I'm sure I'm hurt somewhere!"

Miraculously, I wasn't hurt anywhere! After making sure no bones were broken, Tom pried my arms from the trunk of that tree, and we eventually made it down the mountain. I loved my tree, but I had to let it go. Tom and the kids coaxed me on down, "Come on, Mama! Let's go!"

The choice is yours: Tom McCoy is certainly not the best picture of God in the illustration I've stretched to make my point, but he does lend himself to a loose picture of what God is like.

I don't know what your "tree" looks like, but if you have been clinging to a tree that has gotten you completely off the path God has chosen for you, be sure of this one truth: God will meet you there.

While I clung to my tree, Tom patiently side-stepped his way back up the hill to pluck me from my evergreen friend. No matter where you are, God will meet you there. If you are addicted to prescription drugs, God will meet you there. If you are an alcoholic, God is there. Perhaps you're addicted to day-time television, the internet, or romance novels. God is there. Maybe you know you're pregnant and you're not married—God's been there many times before and He'll be there again. In an affair? God is there. Betrayed a friend? God is there too. In fact, there is no place you could possibly find yourself that God hasn't been before; nor a place He's not willing to go again. Prison, streets, slums, or penthouse—God will meet you there.

MEET ME AT THE MANGER . . .

1. Perhaps you find yourself today desperate for God to rescue you. Let go of your "tree" and trust His love.

2. Read Matthew 1:24. Consider the courage, and the faith, required of Joseph to take Mary as his wife. Ask God to increase your courage and your faith too.

PRAY THIS PRAYER: *Have mercy on me, O God; have mercy on me, for in You my soul takes refuge. I will take refuge in the shadow of Your wings until the disaster has passed. I cry out to God Most High, to God, who fulfills His purpose for me (Psalm 57:1-2). Amen*

CHAPTER 29

PERFECT TIMING

...and she gave birth to her firstborn, a son.
She wrapped him in cloths and placed him in a manger,
because there was no room for them in the inn.
Luke 2:7

Mary is perhaps the most remarkable woman in the barn that night. In fact, she might have been the only woman in the barn that night! However, I think that Mary and Joseph were not alone...I think that if the innkeeper let them stay there, he might have allowed others to stay there too. I imagine that unlike our sweet nativity scenes the barn was most likely noisy and packed full of smelly animals and weary travelers. It was not exactly the kind of private place you might want to have a baby.

Not only that—but having been pregnant three times, and having traveled while I was expecting each of my children, I know that when we have babies, the doctors like for us to stay home the last four weeks of our pregnancies so that we will be close when the time comes. I've no doubt that riding so many grueling miles on a donkey might have initiated her labor!

And all kidding aside, have you ever stopped to realize that God brought hundreds of people to Bethlehem at that time in history to get Mary to Bethlehem to give birth to Jesus? Jesus had to be born in Bethlehem to fulfill the prophecies. There were hundreds of prophecies written in the Old Testament concerning Jesus. And every single one of those prophecies was fulfilled. What are the odds of that?

"Mathematician Peter W. Stoner calculated that probability of one person fulfilling not all the messianic predictions of the Bible…but just eight…He found that the probability would be 1 in 10 to the 17th power, or 1 in 100,000,000,000,000,000. The likelihood of this occurring is comparable to covering Texas with 10 to the 17th power silver dollars, marking only one of them, stirring the mass of dollars, and then having a blindfolded man randomly pick up the marked silver dollar. This is the likelihood of Jesus of Nazareth randomly fulfilling only eight of the Messianic prophecies of the Hebrew Bible."

(quoted from an article *"What does the Hebrew Bible say about the coming Messiah?"* by Michael Rydelnik on pp. 1,352-53 in the Apologetics Study Bible)

Proverbs 19:21 says, "Many are the plans in a man's heart, but it is the Lord's purpose that prevails." God's plans are fulfilled—even if He moves the world to accomplish them! I find great security in that truth.

Meet me at the manger . . .

1. Has God given you a promise He has yet to fulfill? How can you know that He will do it?

2. What plans do you have that need to be surrendered to God's purpose?

3. Underline 2 Corinthians 1:20 in your Bible. Say aloud, "All God's promises are YES!"

Pray this prayer: *Father thank You for the promises in Your Word. Thank You for the assurance that if You've given me Your Word on a particular situation it is as good as done because You keep Your Word. Help me to bring glory to You by trusting You as I patiently wait for You to fulfill Your promise to me. Amen*

CHAPTER 30

HOW?

*In the sixth month, God sent the angel Gabriel to Nazareth,
a town in Galilee, to a virgin pledged to be married to a man
named Joseph, a descendant of David. The virgin's name
was Mary. The angel went to her and said, "Greetings,
you who are highly favored! The Lord is with you."
Mary was greatly troubled at his words and wondered what
kind of greeting this might be. But the angel said to her,
"Do not be afraid, Mary, you have found favor with God.
You will be with child and give birth to a son, and you are to
give him the name Jesus. He will be great and will be called
the Son of the Most High. The Lord God will give him the
throne of his father David, and he will reign over the house of
Jacob forever; his kingdom will never end."
"How will this be," Mary asked the angel,
"since I am a virgin?" The angel answered, "The Holy Spirit
will come upon you, and the power of the Most High will
overshadow you. So the holy one to be born will be called the
Son of God. Even Elizabeth your relative is going to have a
child in her old age, and she who was said to be barren is in
her sixth month. For nothing is impossible with God."
"I am the Lord's servant," Mary answered.
"May it be to me as you have said." Then the angel left her.*

Luke 1:26-38

"...I am the Lord's servant," Mary answered. *"May it be to me as you have said."*

Wow! A young girl, willing to become pregnant outside of marriage— to risk ridicule, and perhaps rejection—and all she wonders is "how?"

"'How will this be,' Mary asked the angel, 'since I am a virgin?'" (Luke 1:34)

That one question is enough to make me want to sit on the porch swing the rest of the afternoon and ponder. I can think of so many questions Mary *could* have asked. Questions like:

- Why me?
- Why now?
- Why not someone else?
- Do you have any idea what agreeing to this is going to cost me? (I'm sure Mary could not have comprehended the answer to that one!)
- What will I say when people start talking?
- Who will take care of me?
- What about Joseph?

You get the idea! I'm beginning to understand that Mary was not called "blessed" because she gave birth to Jesus but because she had such a pure heart and innocent faith before God. Mary's response to Gabriel was not... Why me? Why now? Why not someone else? She didn't argue with God about how difficult this partnership would be—she merely said, "Okay."

MEET ME AT THE MANGER . . .

1. I've always had a habit of noticing the mother of a newborn when I visit them in the hospital. I want to see how she is doing. Imagine you are in the stable with Jesus. Pause for a moment at the manger of Christ and take a look at Mary. How's she doing?

2. Has God ever called you to do something that made no sense at all? What was your response?

3. What would have to happen in you in order to say to God, "I am the Lord's servant, may it be to me as you have said"?

PRAY THIS PRAYER: *Oh Lord, Mary humbles me—her innocent question of curiosity and willingness to be used powerfully in Your plan. Grow in me a heart like Mary's; one that is willing to yield myself completely to Your purpose. Amen*

CHAPTER 31

MARY AND ELIZABETH

*At that time Mary got ready and hurried to a town
in the hill country of Judea, where she entered
Zechariah's home and greeted Elizabeth.*
Luke 1:39

As soon as Mary could get out of town she headed to the mountains to stay with her cousin Elizabeth. Gabriel planted this idea in her mind,

*And consider your relative Elizabeth—even she has
conceived a son in her old age, and this is the sixth month
for her who was called barren. For nothing is impossible with
God. (Luke 1:36-37 HCSB)*

I love this part of the story. Mary's visit with Elizabeth illustrates God's tender mercy and compassion. Elizabeth was an older, wiser, pastor's wife. She was mature in her faith and wise in the ways of the world. After years of prayer most likely accompanied by salty tears, Elizabeth and Zechariah's heart cry was answered. Their infertility ended and John was conceived. It's a funny story of charades and sweet surprise that God gave this faithful couple. (Read it in Luke 1.)

As the reality of Mary's pregnancy set in, she needed a safe place to hide. I can't even imagine what might have taken place in Mary's hometown when the news broke about her pregnancy. But in contrast to what was most likely a stressful, emotionally charged environment at home, when Mary arrived at Elizabeth's house, there was peace and joy.

When Elizabeth heard Mary's greeting, the baby leaped inside her, and Elizabeth was filled with the Holy Spirit. Then she exclaimed with a loud cry: "You are the most blessed of women, and your child will be blessed!" (Luke 1:41-42 HCSB)

Elizabeth was several months ahead of Mary in her pregnancy with John and was therefore able to reassure her during morning sickness. I can almost imagine Elizabeth with a hand on Mary's shoulders pressing a damp cloth across her forehead as Mary let go of her breakfast.

Not only did Elizabeth minister to Mary's physical needs, she most certainly ministered to her emotional and spiritual needs as well. When Elizabeth saw Mary, she believed her incredible story and rejoiced with her in the amazing assignment God had trusted her with.

"How could this happen to me, that the mother of my Lord should come to me? For you see, when the sound of your

greeting reached my ears, the baby leaped for joy inside me!
She who believed is blessed because what was spoken to her by
the Lord will be fulfilled!" (Luke 1:43-45 HCSB)

I've no doubt Elizabeth saw to it that Mary was received well with her family and friends—and that not a
negative word was spoken in her presence. Mary was safe
with Elizabeth.

MEET ME AT THE MANGER . . .

1. Have you ever known someone who ministered to you
physically, emotionally, and spiritually? Thank God for
that person!

2. Perhaps you are that person to someone else. Who
might you encourage?

PRAY THIS PRAYER: *Father, thank You for providing me*
with encouragement from others. Help me to be an encourager
to others. I want to see what You are doing and join You in
Your work by taking care of those You've chosen to use. Today
I pray for [missionaries, faithful servants, pastors, etc.] Amen

CHAPTER 32

THE HEART OF MARY

And Mary said: "My soul glorifies the Lord and my spirit
rejoices in God my Savior, for he has been mindful of
the humble state of his servant. From now on all generations
will call me blessed, for the Mighty One has done
great things for me—holy is his name.
His mercy extends to those who fear him, from generation to
generation. He has performed mighty deeds with his arm; he
has scattered those who are proud in their inmost thoughts.
He has brought down rulers from their thrones but has lifted
up the humble. He has filled the hungry with good things
but has sent the rich away empty. He has helped his servant
Israel, remembering to be merciful to Abraham and his
descendants forever, even as he said to our fathers."

Luke 1:46-55

In the security of Elizabeth's home we capture the song of Mary's heart and understand why God chose her. When many of us might have whined and complained about this role we'd been asked to play, Mary chose to see the bigger picture. She looked beyond her lifetime, and saw how, throughout the generations, we would all call her blessed! Mary believed that God was coming to earth in the person of Jesus—her very own baby boy.

When Mary said, "I am the Lord's servant, may it be to me as you have said," she gave God her life—no agenda of her own, no ambition or plan...just simply willing to be used as He saw fit.

Consider how great a price Mary paid. Not only did she have the pain of traveling to Bethlehem at the end of her pregnancy—and the inconvenience of giving birth to Jesus in a cave/barn! But as He grew from a tiny infant to a toddler and then a boy, she had the wonderful privilege of being His mother. Of picking Him up when He fell—of wiping His tears when He cried, of worrying over Him when they left Him at the temple—and of watching Him become the man of God that He was.

All of that is good and fine. Mary even went on to have other children. But, can you imagine watching your son die the way Jesus died?! The baby you felt turn back flips in your womb; the one who nursed at your breast; the little boy, curious and loving, who in His pre-adolescence had an insatiable appetite for God's Word—the young man who worked hard, and yet always had time to listen to her ponderings...this man, in the prime of His life, never having sinned, all alone, tortured and crucified.

I'm more amazed that Mary was at the foot of the cross than I am that she was in the stable.

MEET ME AT THE MANGER . . .

1. When did you respond to God's call in your life?

2. Have you ever surrendered your whole life to Him?

PRAY THIS PRAYER: *Oh Lord, I am humbled by Mary's complete surrender to Your plan. I'm grateful that You didn't tell her about the cross. Thank You for calling us to partner with You in Your kingdom work and for sustaining us in that partnership. Amen*

CHAPTER 33

A DEFINITION OF SURRENDER

*"I am the Lord's servant," Mary answered.
"May it be to me as you have said."*
Luke 1:38

Wow! That's all I can say about Mary.

I think that Mary—more than any other woman in all God's Word—exemplifies a woman totally sold out, surrendered to God.

"...I am the Lord's servant," Mary answered, "may it be to me as you have said."

How many of us are willing to say that? How many of us are willing to lay aside our own agendas, plans, and ambitions to relinquish our lives—no strings attached to God and His purposes? How many of us are willing to see beyond our own lives to the great plans of God—and be content to play our small part in His great scheme of things?

Too many of us see our life's purpose as being confined to here and now. We limit our contribution to what we do that impacts the world during the tiny window of time that we occupy. But God's purposes are much larger than the brief span of our lives.

David understood this when he wrote,

As a father has compassion on his children, so the Lord has compassion on those who fear Him. For He knows what we are made of, remembering that we are dust. As for man, his days are like grass—he blooms like a flower of the field; when the wind passes over it, it vanishes, and its place is no longer known. (Psalm 103:13-16 HCSB)

God's plan is much larger than our lives. When we are willing to remove ourselves from the center of our world then, and only then, will we be able to surrender our lives to Him.

Mary's heart was surrendered. Therefore she experienced Christmas more intimately and more powerfully perhaps than any other human being.

MEET ME AT THE MANGER . . .

1. Underline Luke 2:38. Then go to John 19 and read the entire chapter.

2. How many of us are willing to say what Mary said in Luke 2:38? How many of us are willing to lay aside our own agendas, plans, and ambitions to relinquish our lives—no strings attached—to God and His purposes? How many of us are willing to see beyond our own lives to the great plans of God—and be content to play our small part in His great scheme of things?

PRAY THIS PRAYER: *I am the Lord's servant, may it be to me as You have said. Amen*

CHAPTER 34

FAVOR IN THE EYES OF GOD

Do not be afraid, Mary, you have found favor with God.
Luke 1:30

Mary found favor with God because her young life already exhibited firm reliance, faith, devotion, and righteousness. The favor of God was based on who Mary was—and what God was inviting her to do. Gabriel greeted her that day with this statement, "Do not be afraid, Mary, you have found favor with God" (Luke 1:30).

How might we find favor with God today? How might we be invited to partner with Him in His kingdom purposes and plans? If you read Genesis 6:8 you will discover another person who "found favor with God."

But Noah found favor in the eyes of the Lord. (Genesis 6:8)

If you study Genesis 6:9 carefully you will discover what characteristics are exhibited in a man or woman who finds favor with God.

This is the account of Noah. Noah was a righteous man, blameless among the people of his time, and he walked with God. (Genesis 6:9)

To walk with God, in cadence with His Word, in stark contrast to ways of the world—that is what qualifies one to find favor with God.

I love Jeremiah 29:11, "For I know the plans I have for you," declares the Lord, "plans to prosper you and not to harm you, plans to give you hope and a future."

This is my life verse. I became acquainted with this verse when I was a teen. When I first read the words, my initial response was, "Great! God has a plan for me!" It was exciting to think that the Lord of all creation cared enough about me to have plans for my life. And for the longest time I pursued that plan.

But this is how I pursued it: God has a plan for MY life! A plan to prosper ME and not to harm ME to give ME a hope and a future!

Can you see how I took the promise of Jeremiah 29:11 and placed myself in the middle of it?

MEET ME AT THE MANGER . . .

1. If Mary had memorized Jeremiah 29:11, how might she have felt when she gave birth to Jesus in a barn?

2. Were the plans God had for Mary easy? Did His plans involve Mary's suffering?

3. How have you considered Jeremiah 29:11 in your own life?

PRAY THIS PRAYER: *Lord, I'm glad You have a plan for my life. The older I get the more I realize that although they are good plans, full of hope and prosperity for me, that doesn't mean they are without pain and suffering. Help me to trust You even when Your plans seem to take me places I'd rather not go. Amen*

CHAPTER 35

JEREMIAH 29:11

"For I know the plans I have for you," declares the Lord,
"plans to prosper you and not to harm you,
plans to give you hope and a future."

Jeremiah 29:11

It took me several years and lots of life experiences to realize that a me-centered interpretation of Jeremiah 29:11 was not at all what God had in mind when He spoke these words to Jeremiah.

First of all, this verse was not written to me. It was written as a promise to the people of Israel—God's chosen people, His precious children, those who fulfilled His covenant relationship with Abraham. The original context of this verse is prophecy.

So let's consider the cultural context of this promise. Jeremiah fulfilled his ministry during the final 40 years proceeding Judah's fall into captivity to the Babylonians. Much of his book deals with the pending disaster and God's desire for Israel to understand that the Babylonian takeover would be punishment for their rejection of the covenant they had with Him.

The specific responsibilities of Israel's covenant relationship with God are recorded in Deuteronomy 27 and

28. Deuteronomy 27:9 says, "*Then Moses, and the priests, who are Levites, said to all Israel, 'Be silent, O Israel, and listen! You have now become the people of the Lord your God. Obey the Lord your God and follow his commands and decrees that I give you today.'*"

Deuteronomy 28:1 says, "*If you fully obey the Lord your God and carefully follow all his commands I give you today, the Lord your God will set you high above all nations on earth.*"

Then the verses that follow in Deuteronomy 28:2-14 describe the incredible blessings promised the Israelites as a result of their choosing to live within the boundaries (limits) set by their call (to be the people of God).

Following a list of the blessings is a serious warning. Deuteronomy 28:15 says, "*However, if you do not obey the Lord your God, and do not carefully follow all his commands and decrees I am giving you today, all these curses will come upon you and overtake you.*"

And then Moses went into great detail regarding the various ways these curses would be executed against them in Deuteronomy 28:16-68. One particularly interesting verse is Deuteronomy 28:49, "*The Lord will bring a nation against you from far away, from the ends of the earth, like an eagle swooping down, a nation whose language you will not understand…*"

This verse from Deuteronomy points to the moment in time that Jeremiah was called to prophesy.

MEET ME AT THE MANGER . . .

1. God has always communicated His purposes to His people—even when they refused to listen. God still insisted on sending prophets to speak His Word. Do you listen to the voice of God today?

2. When you choose to embrace the plans of God, He promises great reward. How has God rewarded your obedience to His Word?

3. When you choose to ignore or blatantly disregard the plans of God He guarantees consequences and punishment. Has God allowed you to suffer for your disobedience? Do you know someone who needs to be reminded of this?

PRAY THIS PRAYER: *Lord, thank You for having great plans for my life. Thank You for calling me to Yourself. Please tune my heart to understand and embrace Your plans. I want to live in the center of Your blessings rather than in the discipline of disobedience. Amen*

CHAPTER 36

GOD'S PLANS ARE HIS OWN

"For I know the plans I have for you…"
Jeremiah 29:11

Much of Jeremiah's book is written to Israel to explain why Israel is about to be punished, and what all that punishment would entail. However, God did not want His people to think they'd been abandoned (even though they had already abandoned God). So, He allowed Jeremiah a glimpse into what was to come after their Babylonian captivity. Jeremiah 29:10 puts the promise of verses 11-14 in historical context:

This is what the Lord says: "When seventy years are completed for Babylon, I will come to you and fulfill my gracious promise to bring you back to this place. For I know the plans I have for you," declares the Lord…

After the inevitable doom, and punishment Israel would receive for her sins, she would once again experience redemption. And that begins the promise that I like to claim for my life verse.

So, you might ask me, "What does all this background information have to do with Jeremiah 29:11 and the application of that promise to my life today?" I'm glad you asked. Although this verse was not written specifically to you, the God who promised is the same One you serve today. And when you put yourself in the context of the passage, the working of His love will extend to you just as it extended to Israel when Jeremiah wept over her coming destruction.

1. God has plans for you. Ephesians 2:10 reinforces this truth: *For we are God's workmanship, created in Christ Jesus to do good works, which God prepared in advance for us to do.*

2. Those plans **are** to prosper you, to give you a hope and a future. Romans 8:28 tells you that even when circumstances seem to rob you of prosperity and hope, God assures you—He is still on His throne, and His plans remain for your good: *And we know that in all things God works for the good of those who love him, who have been called according to his purpose.*

3. But here's the important thing: They are God's plans and not your own!

The plans God has for you are for your good and His glory! They are plans that impact His larger plan.

MEET ME AT THE MANGER . . .

1. Has God revealed to you the good work He prepared in advance for you to do?

2. If so, have you participated in that work?

3. Underline Ephesians 2:10 and Romans 8:28 in your copy of God's Word.

PRAY THIS PRAYER: *Lord, help me to discover the good work You had in mind when You decided to multiply the DNA that created me. Help me to understand the fact that "all things work for my good when I love and trust You. Thank You for having a plan for me; I want to follow You every step of the way. Amen*

CHAPTER 37

IT'S JUST NOT ABOUT YOU

The grass withers and the flowers fall, because
the breath of the Lord blows on them.
Surely the people are grass. The grass withers
and the flowers fall, but the word of God stands forever.

Isaiah 40:7-8

We are on this earth for only a fraction of time—we take up only a fraction of space. God has a great big plan unfolding that began "In the beginning" and will conclude with "Amen." He rules the Universe, and in His good pleasure He chose to create you. You were created to be loved by God, and to fulfill the work He prepared in advance for you to do. Only when you acknowledge Him as Lord, and choose to live within the boundaries of your relationship with Him, will you fully embrace the truth of Jeremiah 29:11.

I was standing next to the Buffalo River in Linden, TN, when this truth penetrated my heart. The river I was watching was flowing powerfully with muddy water. The Buffalo River floods often, and when it floods it makes a mess. I was thinking about my life and the plans I thought God had for me. As I watched that river I realized that I had considered God's plans for my life like a little creek trickling along its merry way doing its own thing for 20, 40, maybe even 80 years or so if I live that long. My little creek contribution to the world would then disappear and all would be gone.

But as I watched the river flow, I began to understand that God's plan is much larger than my limited life. His plan is more like a river. I could jump in that river and float for a bit. I could be swept up in the flow of the river, and could possibly even build a dam and alter its course. But I could never stop it from going where it was determined to go.

I realized that God's plan is like that. He doesn't wait for me to arrive on the scene, grow up, and eventually surrender to Him so that He can quickly get a whole lot of things done that He's been waiting all my life to do. No! God simply moves forward in the powerful flow of His might, and when I decide to participate with Him He invites me to jump in and enjoy the ride.

MEET ME AT THE MANGER . . .

1. In what ways are you tempted to place yourself in the spotlight where God's plans are concerned?

2. How might you shift your focus from yourself to God?

PRAY THIS PRAYER: *Oh God reveal to me the many ways I still try to be the center of attention. I want to be like Mary— able to see the bigger picture and willing to participate with You in that work. Amen*

CHAPTER 38

LIVING FOR
THE GLORY OF GOD

*And Mary said, "My soul glorifies the Lord and my spirit
rejoices in God my Savior."*
Luke 1:46-47

Mary sang her song of praise in Luke 1:46-55 because she lived her life to bring glory to God. If we're not careful we spend our lives looking for God's plan to feature us. We ask God "what do You have for me today?" And what we really mean is "what way do You plan to use *me* in Your kingdom work for *my* good and *my* glory?" Without realizing it, we often bump God out of the limelight and put ourselves in the "star" role of the drama called, "My Life." Too often we offer God the supporting role in this drama, with His sole purpose being to make sure we come out looking good.

This is not what the Bible teaches—not ever. Not even for those who "found favor with God." Neither Mary nor Noah were the featured players in God's plans.

Consider Noah. Scripture says that Noah found favor with God (Genesis 6:3). So God asked Noah to partner with Him in His plan. Noah's role in the flood was the supporting role. He was not the star. Yes, he built the ark (but he didn't design it). Yes, he loaded all the animals on to the ark (but he didn't close the door), and he survived the flood thus preserving life. However it was God who caused the flood, it was God who kept the ark afloat, it was God who sustained life cooped up in the floating zoo, and it was God who made the waters subside. In all actuality, Noah simply walked daily with God and did as he was told. You can read Noah's story in Genesis 6.

God certainly has a plan for your life too. But, it isn't about you. God's plan is about Him. He performs for His own glory, not for ours. God chooses to use those who "walk with Him" to take care of the details of His plan in the world today. In Genesis 6:9 says that "Noah was a righteous man, blameless in his time; Noah walked with God."

Could the same be said of you? Would you be willing to lay aside your list of expectations and desires? Would you be willing to step aside—out of the spotlight, and embrace the role of supporting actor or actress? Would you dedicate your life to making Jesus look good to others? If so, tell God today.

MEET ME AT THE MANGER . . .

1. How might you honor God and celebrate His plans this week?

2. How can you rededicate yourself and your family to "walk with Him"?

PRAY THIS PRAYER: *Father, You are my God, my Savior, my Redeemer and Friend. But You are also my King, my Ruler, and my Lord. I choose to lay aside my own desires [be specific]; I choose to step out of the spotlight and embrace my role of supporting Your plan. I dedicate my life to making You known to everyone I come in contact with. Amen*

CHAPTER 39

THE ANGELS

An angel of the Lord appeared to them, and the glory
of the Lord shone around them, and they were terrified.
But the angel said to them, "Do not be afraid. I bring you
good news of great joy that will be for all people."

Luke 2:9-10

It would be fun to know how many of us have ever played the part of the angels in a Christmas pageant. If you couldn't be Mary, that was the next best role. There was something exciting about standing above everyone else wearing a halo made of tinsel and angel wings constructed from coat hangers and panty hose. Then, when all the others had to be quiet, you were the one who got to shout loud,

"Do not be afraid!
For I bring you good news of great joy!"

We loved playing the part of the angels, didn't we? Can you imagine what the real angels felt like? I did a study on angels and discovered this:

• Angels were created by God—most likely before "the beginning." (Psalm 148:2, 5; Colossians 1:16)

- Scripture tells us that they are stronger and wiser than man. (Jesus implied they had supernatural knowledge in Matthew 24:36 but not unlimited knowledge. Their supernatural power is referenced in 2 Peter 2:11.)

- There are thousands of them (many times in Scripture this is mentioned: Deuteronomy 33:2, Psalm 68:17, Matthew 26:53, Hebrews 12:22, Revelation 5:11 just to name a few).

- They have spiritual bodies and they inhabit spiritual realms—as opposed to earthly bodies that inhabit earthly realms created for us. But they do take on the form of human bodies when sent on human errands (Gabriel with Zechariah and Mary, the angel who proclaimed God's message to the shepherds, and the angel at the tomb).

- Their purposes include:

  ¤ Praising and glorifying God (all the time at the throne of God: Revelation 5:11-12, 7:11, 8:1-4).

  ¤ Revealing and communicating God's message to man (Luke 1:13-20 and 62-38, Acts 8:26, 10:3-7, 11:13, 12:7-11, and 27:23).

◻ Ministering to believers (includes protection but mostly ministering to spiritual needs. (Luke 15:10 and 16:22, Hebrews 1:14, 1 Corinthians 4:9 and 11:10, 1 Timothy 5:21)

◻ Executing judgment on the enemies of God.

◻ Being involved in the second coming of Christ.

(Information about angels came from p. 444
Christian Theology Vol. 1, Erickson, Baker Books, 1983.)

This Biblical description of angels doesn't sound anything like the little cupids that flit about on Valentine's Day does it? Angels are mighty beings that constitute the army of the living God! They are very real, very active, and very present in the Christmas story. Theirs was a significant assignment at the birth of Christ.

Some people think that when we die we become angels. But that will never be. Angels were created by God as an entirely different being. They are stronger and wiser than we, there are lots of them, and they are intent on executing the purposes of God. We can only mimic them as we strive to respond to God's command as obediently as they respond.

MEET ME AT THE MANGER . . .

1. Imagine you are in heaven and God is speaking to His heavenly hosts about the birth of Jesus. What is the atmosphere like?

2. What message might God entrust with you if He were sure you would deliver it just right?

PRAY THIS PRAYER: *Father, thank You for creating the angels. I find comfort in knowing there is a heavenly host engaged in spiritual battle on my behalf. I know that I'm not as strong nor am I as wise as they are, but I want to be obedient. I want to deliver Your message well with boldness and power. Amen*

CHAPTER 40

ONE MORE PERSON IN THE NATIVITY

The Word became flesh and made his dwelling among us.
We have seen his glory, the glory of the One and Only,
who came from the Father, full of grace and truth.

John 1:14

There is one more figure in my nativity scene—it's the smallest one there, but nonetheless my favorite—the newborn baby Jesus.

My daughter Mikel still likes to arrange our nativity scenes. We have them in the bathrooms, the bedrooms, the playroom, living room, kitchen, and even the foyer. She no longer circles the figures around the baby Jesus, but she still lovingly places them in what she considers their proper places. I still giggle when I remember how she had them all circled around that baby in the manger. I thought this was perfect! For Jesus ought to be at the very center of this holiday.

Consider the heart of Jesus—His is a heart of Love.

John 3:16 says, "For God so loved the world that He gave His one and only Son, that whoever believes in Him shall not perish but have eternal life."

Jesus was at His birthday because His Father loved the world. Philippians tells us that Jesus left the splendor of heaven and took on the lowly form of a human—a baby at that!

Your attitude should be the same as that of Christ Jesus: Who, being in the very nature God, did not consider equality with God something to be grasped, but made himself nothing, taking the very nature of a servant, being made in human likeness. And being found in appearance as a man, he humbled himself and became obedient to death—even death on a cross!

Therefore God highly exalted him to the highest place and gave him the name that is above every name, that at the name of Jesus every knee should bow, in heaven and on earth and under the earth, and every tongue confess that Jesus Christ is Lord, to the glory of God the Father. (Philippians 2:5-11)

God hurled Himself into this world at the mercy of those He chose to be His mother and earthly Dad. Think about that! To be the Lord God, Almighty—the Creator of all that was and is and is to come...to be worshipped day and night in the splendor of heaven and then to choose to leave all that...and come to live with us. The Creator choosing to become the created!

...the Word became flesh and dwelt among us. (John 1:14)

Do you realize how powerful that is?! God chose to reveal Himself to us—by becoming like us—for the main purpose of redeeming us! As an infant He had His diapers changed, Mary burped Him, and He most likely suffered rashes, runny noses, and teething. "He made Himself nothing."

And He wants us to be like Him. God's purpose for us today is for us to make Him known among our family members, our co-workers, our friends, our neighbors, and even to those we do not know as we stretch our hearts around the globe. Love compelled God to give...and love compels us to do the same.

MEET ME AT THE MANGER . . .

1. How does it make you feel when you realize the humility Jesus embraced to take on the form of a man?

2. What form of humility does God want you to embrace in order to lead others to Him?

PRAY THIS PRAYER: *Oh Lord, how I bow down in awe of You. Especially when I already know the rest of Your story— how You came to live with us, to love us, and to teach us only to be beaten, whipped, and finally crucified by us. You amaze me with Your love. Please tell me what I can do for You. Amen*

CHAPTER 41

WHAT WAS DIFFERENT ABOUT THOSE WHO CAME?

…and we beheld his glory, glory as of the only begotten of the Father, full of grace and truth.
John 1:14 NASB

There was definitely something different about those who came. There was something unusual about those who came to the stable to see the Christ child—that first holy night; something that allowed them to experience God's work on the earth.

The shepherds were faithful in the ordinary—and willing to believe the extraordinary…so they experienced Christmas.

The wise men were searching for truth—and willing to allow God to show them truth outside their preconceived notions of what it might look like…so they experienced Christmas.

Joseph believed. And because he believed, he was willing to follow God's plan even though it cost him his name and his reputation. He served God by protecting and providing for His Son…so Joseph experienced Christmas.

Mary surrendered her life to God—she was willing to look beyond her own comfort, plans, and goals to be totally at the beck and call of God...so Mary experienced Christmas.

The angels did what they were created to do and Jesus obeyed the will of His Father—so they experienced Christmas.

Will you experience Christmas?

MEET ME AT THE MANGER . . .

1. Which of the characters in the nativity scene can you most identify with?

2. Ask God to make you like that one so that you can be aware of His activity in your world today.

PRAY THIS PRAYER: *Lord, I want to really experience Christmas like these men and women experienced Christmas. I want to "be there" with You where You are. I want to have my heart in tune with Yours. I want to hear the angels sing "Glory to God in the highest and on earth, peace and good will to men." Amen*

CHAPTER 42

DON'T MISS CHRISTMAS

So they hurried off and found Mary and Joseph,
and the baby, who was lying in a manger.
Luke 2:16

So much of our Christmas celebration is defined for us through magazines, movies, and malls. But as a child of God you know what is really worth celebrating. This year don't miss Christmas.

Like the shepherds, be faithful.
Be very careful, then, how you live—not as unwise but as wise, making the most of every opportunity, because the days are evil. Therefore do not be foolish, but understand what the Lord's will is. (Ephesians 5:15-17)

Like the wise men, be truth-seekers.
Then you will know the truth, and the truth will set you free. (John 8:32)

Like Joseph, be a believer.
Yet, I am not ashamed, for I know Whom I have believeth, and am persuaded that He is able, to keep that which I've committed unto Him against that day. (2 Timothy 1:12 KJV)

146

Like Mary, be completely surrendered.

I have been crucified with Christ and I no longer live, but Christ lives in me. The life I live in the body, I live by faith in the Son of God, who loved me and gave Himself for me. (Galatians 2:20)

Like the angels, fulfill God's purpose for you.

"For I know the plans I have for you," declares the Lord, "plans to prosper you and not to harm you. Plans to give you a hope and a future." (Jeremiah 29:11)

Like Jesus, embrace humility.

And being found inappearance as a man he humbled himself and became obedient to death—even death on a cross! (Philippians 2:8)

I hope that you will put at least one nativity scene in your home this holiday season. And, when you do, I hope that you will pause and ponder why these were the ones who took time to notice God was up to something big—and then to worship Him.

MEET ME AT THE MANGER . . .

1. Is God up to something big in your family? In your church? Your community? How can you be sure to recognize Him at work?

2. Put aside an evening and watch a version of the Nativity on DVD as a family. Consider the hearts of those who gathered on the first Christmas Day. Allow God to work into you a heart like theirs.

PRAY THIS PRAYER: *Father, I want to be one who hears the angels sing. I want to see Your star and come to bow before You as often as You call to me. Thank You for inviting me into Your presence. Father, we are Your servants. Each of us have families and friends to love. We have people in our lives who desperately need to know You, and because we know You, we have the opportunity to share You with others. Make our hearts sensitive to those who need to know You today—and allow us the quiet time this season to worship the Christ child like…the shepherds, the wise men, Joseph and Mary worshipped Him that very first Christmas. We don't want to miss You in the hustle and bustle…use us to usher Your presence and Your love into our homes. In Jesus' precious and powerful name we pray. Amen*

PART 2

UNWRAP THE GIFT
OF HIS PRESENCE

Praise be to the God and Father of our Lord Jesus Christ,
who has blessed us in the heavenly realms
with every spiritual blessing in Christ.

Ephesians 1:3

When God gave us His Son, He gave us the ultimate gift. In these next devotions we will unwrap the gift of His Presence. At Christmas we celebrate the gift of Jesus—the very image of God in the body of man. But when Jesus came to earth, He brought with Him many amazing spiritual blessings, blessings that remain here today for us to enjoy. We would do well to carefully unwrap each one over and over again.

CHAPTER 43

LOTS OF SURPRISES!

*I pray also that the eyes of your heart may be enlightened
in order that you may know the hope to which he has called
you, the riches of his glorious inheritance in the saints,
and his incomparably great power for us who believe.
That power is like the working of His mighty strength.*
Ephesians 1:18-19

I don't know how your family participates in the unwrapping ritual, but we have two family celebrations. At the McCoy family Christmas, we circle up and one grandchild disperses the presents. Each person has several packages in front of them. No one really gives the signal—but somehow everyone knows when to tear into their pile of gifts. So without a cue, wrapping paper and ribbons fly, and everyone talks at the same time. Some squeal with delight, others run around giving hugs, and when the ruckus ends, everyone smiles. When the children were young I was a nervous wreck—trying to make sure that my children appropriately thanked each relative for the coordinating gift.

At the Keesee Christmas, we savor our unwrapping ritual. Each giver goes to the tree and takes one gift from under it. She then gives it to the recipient and sits down.

The recipient oohs and ahhs over the wrapping, the ribbon and the perfect paper, then she (there are lots of "shes" in my family) carefully unwraps the package, saving the bow and sometimes the paper! But she doesn't open the box yet, she shakes it gently and makes guesses much to the delight of the giver. Finally, she opens the package, and goes on and on about the contents. This process begins again with the next gift. While the McCoy ritual lasts about 10 minutes, the Keesee ritual lasts for hours!

When I was a child, my parents asked me what I wanted for Christmas. My list included one big item (a doll or an art easel and painting set or a Barbie dollhouse) and "lots of surprises." How I think of what God gave us on the first Christmas day—He delivered us His Son, and included "lots of surprises." In Ephesians 1 Paul tells us that "in Christ" we have been given many spiritual blessings:

Praise be to the God and Father of our Lord Jesus Christ, who has blessed us in the heavenly realms with every spiritual blessing in Christ. (Ephesians 1:3)

Sometimes we get so busy during this time of year that we totally miss the "surprises" God lavishly poured on us when He gave us Jesus. In these next few days, celebrate His gifts. Either tear into them, squeal with delight, or enjoy the extravagance of His love, or quietly savor the beauty of each one. Unwrap His gifts slowly and ponder the thought that went into its purchase. Unwrap them again and again, and cherish each one anew.

UNWRAP THE GIFT OF HIS PRESENCE...

1. Can you list some of the "surprises" God gave you in Christ? (For help, read Ephesians 1 again.) Thank Him for giving you so much when He gave you His Son.

2. Do you remember what you "got" for Christmas last year? Do your children? Spend some time with your family remembering what you received last year. Discuss the thought and money that went into those gifts. Ask them to think of ways they can show their gratitude this year for the gifts they will receive.

3. Invite your family members to think of ways God has blessed you all this year. Make a list and call these your "Lots of Surprises." Post your list on your refrigerator.

PRAY THIS PRAYER: *Father, thank You for the gift of Your Son. Thank You for every spiritual blessing that accompanied His coming. Help me to focus on those blessings in these next few days—to take time in the busyness of this season to savor the gifts You've given me. Amen*

CHAPTER 44

GOD ALWAYS KEEPS HIS PROMISES

*A voice of one calling: "In the desert prepare the way for the
Lord; make straight in the wilderness a highway for our God.
Every valley shall be raised up, every mountain and hill
made low; the rough ground shall become level, the rugged
places a plain. And the glory of the Lord will be revealed,
and all mankind together will see it.
For the mouth of the Lord has spoken."*

Isaiah 40:3-5

J esus came to give us a "straight way" to God. Many
hundreds of years before the angels sang to the shepherds that "silent night," God whispered in the ear of
His prophet Isaiah—and Isaiah wrote these words.

Several years ago, the highway department in the
state of Tennessee began construction on Interstate
840—a by-pass that currently connects the south to the
east side of Nashville. Eventually the plan is to create a
circle around Nashville in a 35 to 50 mile radius. When
construction began on this road, we watched as a straight
way was made in the wilderness. The construction crews
used dynamite to make the mountains and the hills
low. Concrete pillars lifted up bridges that raised up the

valleys. The rough ground became level, and the rugged places plain; now I can drive 70 mph from the entry point two miles from my front door in Franklin all the way to Lebanon where 840 temporarily ends.

When Isaiah uttered these words, he used the picture of highway construction to explain a spiritual truth: The glory of the Lord would be revealed (in the Person of Jesus Christ). And all mankind would have the opportunity to see the Lord in all His glory (the Word would become flesh, and had we been there with His disciples, we would have beheld His glory).

But in order to witness the glory of the Lord, people needed to be made ready. They needed to have their eyes opened, their ears attuned, their minds alert. So, in fulfillment of Isaiah's prophecy, God sent John (not the apostle, but the Baptist). John's birth was also announced by Gabriel. (Read Luke 1:11-17.)

Zechariah considered this news too good to be true and doubted the angel's words. That's why his voice was taken from him until John's birth. It's kind of a funny story, and you should read it for yourself in Luke 1. But, this part is not funny…it's worth pondering long and hard. What Isaiah prophesied 600 years before, and what Gabriel told Zechariah that day in the temple, came about just as God said it would. Second Corinthians 2:20 says this, *For no matter how many promises God has made, they are "yes" in Christ. And so through him the "Amen" is spoken by us to the glory of God.*

As you celebrate the holidays this year, remember that all God's promises are YES! So, when you choose to take God at His Word—and anchor your hope in Him— you bring glory to God as you testify to your belief. The word "Amen" means, "So be it." How many promises has God given you? How many promises are you waiting on Him to fulfill? They are all "YES" in Christ Jesus! So glorify God by trusting Him.

Unwrap the gift of His presence...

1. Thank God that all His promises are YES!

2. Make a list of the promises God has made to you—and just after each one print this phrase: *I choose to trust You because all Your promises are YES!*

PRAY THIS PRAYER: *Father, thank You for making good on all Your promises. Thank You for being faithful to fulfill Your plans. Oh God, thank You most for sending Jesus—Your precious, perfect Lamb, to pay the penalty for my sin. Thank You for the intimacy we can share today. Amen*

CHAPTER 45

A STRAIGHT WAY TO GOD

In those days John the Baptist came, preaching in the Desert
of Judea and saying, "Repent, for the kingdom of heaven
is near." This is he who was spoken of through the prophet
Isaiah:"A voice of one calling in the desert,
'prepare the way for the Lord, make straight paths for him.'"
John's clothes were made of camel's hair
and he had a leather belt around his waist.
His food was locusts and wild honey. People went out
to him from Jerusalem and all Judea and the whole region of
the Jordan. Confessing their sins,
they were baptized by him in the Jordan River.

Matthew 3:1-6

When Elizabeth gave birth to John, Zechariah received his voice back, and he named his son as the angel had directed. John grew up to fulfill the promise that was given concerning him. Matthew 3 records John's ministry.

John prepared the way for Jesus. He prepared men's hearts by exposing their sin. He called them to repentance. John could not forgive sin—but he could expose it. For those of us who have received forgiveness of our sins, we can do the same. We cannot forgive sin, but we can lovingly share the same message John shared. We can point others toward the One who does.

I baptize you with water for repentance. But after me will come one who is more powerful than I, whose sandals I am not fit to carry. He will baptize you with the Holy Spirit and fire. (Matthew 3:11)

Jesus, not John, provided a straight way to God. He willingly offered Himself as a sacrifice for our sin. He was the spotless "Lamb of God." Jesus paved the way for us to experience intimacy with our Creator. He restored what sin destroyed. Sin buckled the path with mountains, hills, ravines, and valleys. But when Jesus died on the cross, He leveled the mountains, raised the valleys, and paved the way.

John testifies concerning Him. He cries out, saying,
"This was he of whom I said, He who comes after me has
surpassed me because he was before me."
From the fullness of his grace we have all received
one blessing after another.

John 1:15-16

UNWRAP THE GIFT OF HIS PRESENCE...

1. Share with your family your baptism stories. Tell your children where you were, who baptized you, why you chose to be baptized, and what that means to you today. Encourage your children to relive their baptisms too. If you have pictures, bring them out and display them in your home this Christmas season.

2. Reflect on the sacrificial gift of the "Lamb of God." Discuss what this means with your children.

PRAY THIS PRAYER: *Lord, thank You for sending John to prepare the people's hearts for the Lord. Thank You for being the perfect "Lamb of God." Help me to live today grateful for Your sacrifice. Amen*

CHAPTER 46

A REAL RELATIONSHIP WITH GOD

I tell you the truth, we speak of what we know,
and we testify to what we have seen,
but still you people do not accept our testimony.

John 3:11

Perhaps the greatest gift of all is forgiveness of sin, but before people could receive this gift they had to get past the stronghold of religion. Nicodemus' nighttime encounter with Jesus illustrates this truth. When Nicodemus came to Jesus, Jesus challenged him to let go of religious tradition that blinded him from the truth. The following is an excerpt from my Bible study *Learning to Love Surrender*:

When Nicodemus came to Jesus, he was alone. But when he addressed Jesus, he referred to the brotherhood he shared with the Pharisees and the ruling Jewish council (the Sanhedrin) by saying, "we know that you are a teacher…" (see John 3:2). Jesus understood that Nicodemus was speaking on behalf of the Pharisees, but He addressed Nicodemus as an individual first. After Jesus told Nicodemus that he would never understand who He (Jesus) truly was unless he was "born again," He then made reference to Nicodemus' close relationship with the Pharisees by telling Nicodemus that He (Jesus) also shared a close relationship with other men. Jesus used the plural pronoun "we" in verse 11 just like Nicodemus used it in verse 2.

He [Nicodemus] came to Jesus at night and said, "Rabbi, we know you are a teacher who has come from God. For no one could perform the miraculous signs you are doing if God were not with him." (John 3:2)

I tell you the truth, we speak of what we know, and we testify to what we have seen, but still you people do not accept our testimony. (John 3:11)

Consider this as a possible way Jesus was explaining Himself to Nicodemus:

"Nicodemus, your way of thinking has error at its root. You are committed to that way of thinking—you've given your entire life to it. Your belief system drives you. What you think rules the way you live. But I'm telling you that in order to understand WHO I truly am, you've got to think differently. You must completely erase all that you thought was right and entertain new thoughts. You are surrounded by men who think like you think—but who are wrong. I am part of a group of men who have proclaimed TRUTH that Israel's leaders have refused to receive. Just as the prophets were rejected in their days, so also will I be rejected today."

"...We speak of what we know, and we testify to what we have seen, but still (after all this time) you people do not accept our testimony."

Not only did Jesus identify Himself with the prophets whose prophecies were rejected; but He also linked Himself to a brotherhood of men. Just as Nicodemus shared brotherhood with the Pharisees, so Jesus explained that He shared brotherhood with the prophets and His little band of disciples. Jesus did this to woo Nicodemus to wake up from his slumber—a slumber linked to years of tradition and religiosity, a sleep kept deep by the shared confusion of his fellow Pharisees.

Nicodemus had a hard time following Jesus' figurative language. He couldn't process the spiritual revelation of rebirth because Jesus taught outside Nicodemus' bias. Jesus spoke of realities that couldn't be experienced through rote memory and diligent study. Jesus spoke of relationship not religion.

UNWRAP THE GIFT OF HIS PRESENCE...

1. What cultural or religious biases make people spiritually blind today? Are any of these biases in you?

2. Would you characterize your Christian faith as a religion or a relationship? What is the difference?

PRAY THIS PRAYER: *Lord, I want to be like Nicodemus, willing to step away from my friends and seek truth for myself. I want You to give me wisdom and understanding even if that means I have to let go of beliefs I've held tight for many years. Amen*

CHAPTER 47

SPIRITUAL BLINDNESS

For although they knew God, they neither glorified him as God nor gave thanks to him, but their thinking became futile and their foolish hearts were darkened.

Romans 1:21

I was writing my Bible study *Learning to Love Surrender* when this verse literally jumped off the page of my Bible and smacked me on my nose. I was focusing on the power of God in the chapter I was writing, and I'd just gone from Genesis to Romans 1:18-20 to make the point that no man is without excuse before God because His invisible attributes are displayed in His creation.

"The wrath of God is being revealed from heaven against all the godlessness and wickedness of men who suppress the truth by their wickedness, since what may be known about God is plain to them, because God has made it plain to them. For since the creation of the world God's invisible qualities— his eternal power and divine nature—have been clearly seen, being understood from what has been made, so that men are without excuse."

These verses make that truth plain. "For since the creation of the world God's invisible qualities—his eternal power and divine nature—have been clearly seen, being understood from what has been made, so that men are without excuse." Then I read forward and discovered that men who are "without excuse" are also without understanding. But their lack of understanding doesn't come from God. The darkness that covers their hearts results from their own decision to "neither glorify God nor give thanks to Him."

Read Romans 1:21 again.

"For although they [the godless and wicked men who suppress the truth by their wickedness—see verse 18] knew God [because He made Himself plain to them through His creation], they neither glorified him as God [they didn't acknowledge Him as Creator and Sustainer of life] nor gave thanks to him, [they never thanked Him for what He had done for them] …"

Let's pause here. Men have a tendency to neglect God. Many people in our world today walk about as if they just happened to emerge from the muck and evolve into the intelligent, amazing people they are. They never give glory to God by acknowledging His existence much less His sovereignty and love.

UNWRAP THE GIFT OF HIS PRESENCE...

1. Underline Romans 1:21 in your copy of God's Word.

2. Ask God to help you remember the times when you believed Him the best. Relive the joy of those moments.

PRAY THIS PRAYER: *Father, forgive me for neglecting You. Forgive me for taking credit for my good sense, my ability to succeed, for anything at all! Help me to remember that You are my Life. Amen*

CHAPTER 48

EYES WIDE OPEN

When Jesus heard that they had thrown the man out, He
found him and asked, "Do you believe in the Son of Man?"
"Who is He, Sir, that I may believe in Him?" he asked.
Jesus answered, "You have seen Him; in fact,
He is the One speaking with you." "I believe, Lord!"
he said, and he worshiped Him. Jesus said, "I came into this
world for judgment, in order that those who do not see will
see and those who do see will become blind." Some of the
Pharisees who were with Him heard these things and asked
Him, "We aren't blind too, are we?" "If you were blind,"
Jesus told them, "you wouldn't have sin.
But now that you say, 'We see'—your sin remains."

John 9:35-41 HCSB

Consider the man who was born blind at birth. His story is in John 9. Jesus healed this man in an intimate way. He took His own spit, mixed it with dirt, and smeared the mud over the man's eyes. Then He told the man to go wash his eyes in the pool of Siloam. When the blind man went to wash his eyes, Jesus and His disciples evidently went on their way.

However, he did see the Pharisees. They brought him

before the ruling counsel because he was the recipient of a controversial miracle. When John recorded this story he almost forgot to mention that Jesus performed this miracle on the Sabbath. Well, that was obviously breaking the Sabbath law—and the Pharisees had a difficult time understanding why Jesus would do such a thing. Their relentless interrogation of the now-seeing man led to the man's gradual understanding that Jesus was not a mere prophet as he first thought. At the beginning of his interaction with the Pharisees, they asked him to tell them who he thought Jesus was.

Finally they turned again to the blind man, "What have you to say about him? It was your eyes he opened." The man replied, "He is a prophet." (John 9:17)

But after questioning his parents, then begging him to "Give glory to God" by declaring Jesus to be a sinner (I find this ironic—the Pharisees were so confused in their religiosity and pride that they thought they could coerce "glory to God" out of their witness by forcing him to refute Jesus' deity), their exhausting pursuit led to the blind man's spiritual sight.

Nobody has ever heard of opening the eyes of a man born blind. If this man were not from God, he could do nothing. (John 9:33)

When the blind man made that declaration of his budding faith, the Pharisees threw him out of the synagogue—declaring him "steeped in sin from birth."

(Which, by the way, was a traditional belief shared by the Jewish elite. The belief was that if someone was born handicapped either his/her own sin caused the misfortune or the sin of his/her parents caused it. Kind of has an air of self-righteousness for those who were fortunate enough to be born whole, doesn't it?)

Left in his spiritual fog, the "blind man" most likely slipped away someplace to be alone. His head had to be spinning with the sights of a world he'd merely smelled, felt, and heard before. His heart had to be confused by the interesting turn of events he'd experienced this day. And as the man was sorting through his thoughts, Jesus came to him. During this second encounter with Jesus, we see a beautiful picture of what it means to "give glory to God."

Jesus heard that they had thrown him out, and when he found him, he said, "Do you believe in the Son of Man?" "Who is he, sir?" the man asked. "Tell me so that I may believe in him." Jesus said, "You have now seen him; in fact, he is the one speaking to you." Then the man said, "Lord, I believe," and he worshipped him. (John 9:35-38)

The now-seeing man worshipped God when he believed in Him.

UNWRAP THE GIFT OF HIS PRESENCE...

1. This is a great example of the spiritual fog that comes as a result of pride. Invite God to show you any pride that you need to let go.

2. Think of the last time your spiritual eyes were opened. How did you feel?

Pray this prayer: Lord, thank You for refusing to leave me with my eyes half open. Please give me spiritual sight today so that I can see You as You are. Amen

CHAPTER 49

BY FAITH

By faith, Abraham, even though he was past age—and
Sarah herself was barren—was enabled to become a father
because he considered him faithful who made the promise.
And so from this one man, and he as good as dead,
come descendants as numerous as the stars in the sky
and as countless as the sand on the seashore.

Hebrews 11:11-12

Hebrews 11 lists men and women who glorified God with their lives. They acted "by faith." My favorite part of that chapter is the part that speaks of Abraham, the father of our faith. Don't you love the phrase, "…and he as good as dead…"?

Abraham, Jacob, Esau, Joseph, Moses, and all the others gave glory to God by acting "by faith." The writer of Hebrews reminds us that we cannot please God without faith.

And without faith it is impossible to please Him, for he
who comes to God must believe that He is and that He is a
rewarder of those who seek Him. (Hebrews 11:6 NASB)

We give glory to God when we believe Him. Will you give glory to God? Will you respond to God's leadership in your life and live "by faith"? Will you believe He is who He says He is and worship Him?

Be duly warned. When you choose to neglect the glory of God, your thinking will become futile and your heart will be darkened. This is the part of Romans 1:21 that smacked me in the nose.

For although they knew God, they neither glorified him as God nor gave thanks to him, but their thinking became futile and their foolish hearts were darkened. (Romans 1:21)

If you are suffering from confusion, depression, and unexplained anxiety, try giving glory to God. Walk back to the place where you first believed, and relive that moment of truth. Bow down at the feet of Jesus and worship Him.

UNWRAP THE GIFT OF HIS PRESENCE...

1. If you are physically able, get on your knees and bow before God. Imagine Him— the Creator, Ruler, and Giver and Taker of life. Thank Him for being who He is.

2. Consider how you can act on what you believe today.

PRAY THIS PRAYER: *Father, forgive me for failing to take the time to give You glory. I know that You are God—and that You are above all other powers in this world. Thank You for being on Your throne. Lord, I believe You! I trust You, and therefore today I will... Amen*

CHAPTER 50

THANK HIM!

*For although they knew God, they neither glorified him
as God nor gave thanks to him, but their thinking became
futile and their foolish hearts were darkened.*

Romans 1:21

According to Romans 1:21 and the verses that follow, the penalties are severe for those who neglect thanksgiving. First of all, when you don't give thanks (just as when you fail to give God glory), your thinking becomes futile. In other words, your thoughts fall short of any useful purpose. The way you think will lack substance—you'll consider worthless things worthy and valuable things worthless.

Do you see any evidence of futile thinking in America today? What about the "pursuit of happiness" that sends men and women clamoring up the ladder of "success" while their children suffer from parental neglect? How many people have you met who—when it's all said and done—wish they could erase what they said and undo what was done? Failure to give God thanks leads to futile (pointless, fruitless, unsuccessful, ineffective, and wasted) thinking.

Romans 1:21 also tells us that when we fail to glorify God and refuse to give thanks, our hearts are darkened. In fact, when you fail to give God thanks, Paul labels your heart foolish. A foolish heart loves the wrong things. A foolish heart gets its feelings hurt too easily. A foolish heart is driven by emotion.

Read the verses following Romans 1:21 and watch the digression that occurs when we "neither glorify him as God nor give thanks to him."

Although they claimed to be wise, they became fools and exchanged the glory of the immortal God for images made to look like mortal man and birds and animals and reptiles. Therefore God gave them over in the sinful desires of their hearts to sexual impurity for the degrading of their bodies with one another. They exchanged the truth of God for a lie, and worshiped and served created things rather than the Creator— who is forever praised. Amen. Because of this, God gave them over to shameful lusts. Even their women exchanged natural relations for unnatural ones. In the same way the men also abandoned natural relations with women and were inflamed with lust for one another. Men committed indecent acts with other men, and received in themselves the due penalty for their perversion. (Romans 1:22-27)

UNWRAP THE GIFT OF HIS PRESENCE...

1. Give thanks to God! Start right now naming all the things that come to you straight from the hand of God.

2. Play this game with your family—ask, where did the corn come from? (If they say the can, say, "Before that!" And when they say, the grocery store—"Before that!" Then the farm—"Before that!" Go all the way back to the seed, and the soil, the rain and the sun. Then thank God for the corn.

PRAY THIS PRAYER: *Lord, thank You! Thank You for...* *[be specific, exhaustive, and complete] ... Amen*

CHAPTER 51

KNOWLEDGE OF GOD

*Furthermore, since they did not think it worthwhile to retain
the knowledge of God, he gave them over to a depraved
mind, to do what ought not to be done.*

Romans 1:28

Would your grandparents ever have imagined a day when we would have a president who declared in his campaign that he believed same-sex union should be given the same recognition as marriage? Certainly we live in a culture that Paul described! And, where did it all begin? Go back to verse 21 and read again,

*For although they knew God, they neither glorified Him
as God nor gave thanks to him…*

That, my friends is where it started. But unfortunately it doesn't stop yet. Paul has more to say, "Furthermore, since they did not think it worthwhile to retain the knowledge of God, he gave them over to a depraved mind, to do what ought not to be done." (Romans 1:28)

Notice the decay of the mind. First this mind "knew God" (verse 21). Then, because he "neither glorified nor gave thanks to Him" his mind became futile (unsuccessful, fruitless). But after living in futility, God gave his mind over to depravity (immorality, corruption, evil, and wickedness). Not only does a depraved mind "do what ought not to be done," but it also becomes full of all kinds of evil:

They have become filled with every kind of wickedness, evil, greed and depravity. They are full of envy, murder, strife, deceit and malice. They are gossips, slanderers, God-haters, insolent, arrogant and boastful; they invent ways of doing evil; they disobey their parents; [I find it interesting that disobeying parents sits right next to murderers, slanderers and God-haters.] they are senseless, faithless, heartless, ruthless. Although they know God's righteous decree that those who do such things deserve death, they not only continue to do these very things but also approve of those who practice them. (Romans 1:29-32)

This is terrible! It's like a world spinning out of control. It's like the one we live in. But here is the glorious truth; God will turn this terrible destructive cycle around if those of us who know Him will glorify Him and give Him thanks.

UNWRAP THE GIFT OF HIS PRESENCE...

1. Pray for our country. Underline 2 Chronicles 7:14-15. We humble ourselves when we pray. We humble ourselves when we acknowledge God. We humble ourselves when we declare our desperate dependence on Him.

2. We humble ourselves when we give thanks.

PRAY THIS PRAYER: *Oh Lord, forgive us for neglecting You! Thank You for all that You do, but especially for being patient with me. Amen*

CHAPTER 52

FORGIVENESS OF SIN

*For God did not send His Son into the world to condemn
the world, but to save the world through him.*

John 3:17

Had Nicodemus not come to talk to Jesus we
might not have had John 3:16—the most quoted verse in the entire Bible.

"For God so loved the world that He gave His only
begotten Son that whoever believes in him shall not perish but
have eternal life."

But few of us can quote the verses that follow.

*For God did not send his Son into the world to condemn
the world, but to save the world through him. Whoever believes
in him is not condemned, but whoever does not believe stands
condemned already because he has not believed in the name of
God's one and only Son. (John 3:17-8)*

Remember Jesus was talking to Nicodemus—and Nicodemus was a member of the Sanhedrin. One translation of the Bible says, "For God did not send the Son into the world to judge the world…" Judging the world was primarily the passion of the Pharisees. They were adamant about pointing out who could and who could not be accepted by God. The Pharisees also spent hours debating what one must do or must not do in order to live a life of righteousness (to gain favor from God).

Jesus said to Nicodemus, "God did not send me to judge the world—no, my mission is totally opposite of that. God sent Me into the world to save the world."

These two verses teach a critical truth. Jesus' primary mission on earth was to save mankind—not to condemn us. Many people refuse to come to God because they see Him as an angry judge full of condemnation and rebuke. While God is certainly holy, full of righteousness, without any fault at all, He doesn't take pleasure in judging mankind. God's love for us compelled Him to send His Son to us, not to condemn us, but to save us!

"For God so loved that world that He *gave* His only begotten Son."

Jesus explained that all anyone has to do to enter the kingdom of God is believe in Him. If one believes, He is not condemned. If one does not believe, He remains in the condemned state where he already stands. God didn't need to send Jesus here to condemn the world; the world was condemned already. In fact, God sent Jesus here *because* the world was condemned already.

UNWRAPPING THE GIFT OF HIS PRESENCE...

1. Think about the wonder of God's love and the extent of His grace. Thank Him for offering us forgiveness of sin.

2. Do you have family members or friends who consider God a condemning judge? Pray for them right now and ask God to use you to explain how His righteousness was reconciled with His love on the cross.

PRAY THIS PRAYER: *Father, let the truth of Your love penetrate my heart. Give me wisdom in sharing this truth with [name of family member or friend who considers God an angry judge]. Let me be a light that illuminates Your love today. Amen*

CHAPTER 53

HUNGER AND THIRST

Then Jesus declared, "I am the bread of life.
He who comes to me will never go hungry,
and he who believes in me will never be thirsty."

John 6:35

The older I get, the more I enjoy bread! I love to dip bread in olive oil. I enjoy the multigrain "baguettes" served with soup at Panera's. I love pancakes at Cracker Barrel. In Franklin, TN, we have a famous bakery called Meridee's. Often I purchase carrot cakes from Meridee's for Christmas parties I host in my home. I have a dear friend who delivers our family a basket of breads from Meridee's every Christmas season. My children and I look forward to this treat. I love bread!!

In our affluent culture, bread is not a staple. Instead, it is often something to be eaten in moderation or given up altogether (as many on low-carb diets can attest). However, in Jesus' day bread was essential to the diet. The bread Jesus ate was much healthier than the kind we purchase in the grocery. I've tasted His kind of bread. Several years ago my husband had a secretary who grew convicted that she needed to serve her family wholesome bread. She purchased a tool she used to grind her own wheat, and cooked bread without preservatives. Her bread was heavy and filling! It stayed fresh for only a day (maybe 2 if it was refrigerated). This bread did not even begin to resemble the 40-calorie slices I use to make peanut butter and jelly sandwiches I pack in my children's lunches.

In Jesus' day women cooked bread daily. Their bread was like the bread Diane made, and because they didn't have refrigeration, their bread had to be made fresh daily. When Jesus said, "*I am the bread of life*," He was speaking in the context of this kind of bread.

Jesus said to them, "I tell you the truth, it is not Moses who has given you the bread from heaven, but it is my Father who gives you the true bread from heaven. For the bread of God is he who comes down from heaven and gives life to the world." "Sir," they said, "from now on give us this bread."

Then Jesus declared, "I am the bread of life. He who comes to me will never go hungry, and he who believes in me will never be thirsty." (John 6:32-35)

UNWRAP THE GIFT OF HIS PRESENCE...

1. What did Jesus mean when He said, "He who comes to me will never go hungry?"

2. What did Jesus mean when He said, "He who believes in me will never be thirsty?"

PRAY THIS PRAYER: *Father I am rarely ever hungry or thirsty even in the physical sense of the word today. But when I do get hungry and when I am thirsty I recognize the irritation in my body. Let me develop such an appetite for You that I hunger and thirst spiritually in the same way I hunger and thirst physically. Amen*

CHAPTER 54

WHAT IS REAL?

*Jesus then said to them, "Truly, truly, I say to you, it is not
Moses who has given you the bread out of heaven, but it is
My Father who gives you the true bread out of heaven.
"For the bread of God is that which comes down out of
heaven, and gives life to the world." Then they said to Him,
"Lord, always give us this bread." Jesus said to them,
"I am the bread of life; he who comes to Me will not hunger,
and he who believes in Me will never thirst.*
John 6:32-35 NASB

Jesus was speaking to men who'd witnessed His feeding of the 5,000 with five loaves of bread and two fish. The men were eager to see more miraculous signs, and they likened Jesus' picnic miracle with Moses' feeding of the Israelites when they wandered in the desert. (Although Moses didn't feed the Israelites—God did.) For this background information you need to read all of John 6. As Jesus responded to their request for more of His miraculous bread, He used their physical appetites and urged them to allow what was physical to illustrate what was spiritual.

This is a good place to ask this question. What is real? Is the world real? Is your home real? Are people real?

How do you know they are real? You might say, "Yes! The world is real, I can see it—and touch it, smell it, and taste it! People are real, I can see them, touch them, interact with them." Then, let me ask you this question: What remains forever? Does the world? Your home? People? You must answer, "No, my home will not remain forever. People do not remain forever—not on this earth. And even the world is ever-changing and showing signs of decay." Then, would what is real be defined by what can be seen, tasted, heard, and touched? Or, by what remains forever? What is real?

Jesus challenged the people to think larger when He said, "I am the bread of life. He who comes to me will never go hungry, and he who believes in me will never be thirsty." While they were looking for what they could see, taste, touch, and feel, Jesus urged them to embrace what was real—that which was not limited to physical senses.

Would the people who believed in Jesus be hungry again? Physically—yes…spiritually—no.

Would those who believed in Jesus be thirsty again? Physically—yes…spiritually—no.

UNWRAP THE GIFT OF HIS PRESENCE...

1. Satan is the Deceiver. He wants you to believe that what you can see, touch, taste, hear, and feel is what is real. But Jesus says, "I am the Bread of Life. He who comes to Me will never go hungry, and he who believes in Me will never be thirsty." Do you believe Him? Which is the shadow and which is real?

2. Make a list of those things. I've started this list for you:

Shadow	Real
Life on earth	Life after death
Bread	God's Word
Water	Living Water
	(see John 4)

PRAY THIS PRAYER: *Lord, I am so easily deceived. I spend much of my time and energy chasing after things that aren't even real! Help me to believe Your Word. Help me to develop an appetite for the bread of life and living water that You offer me. Amen*

CHAPTER 55

THE BREAD OF LIFE

Then Jesus declared, "I am the bread of life.
He who comes to me will never go hungry,
and he who believes in me will never be thirsty."

John 6:35

In John 6 Jesus challenged His followers just as He challenged Nicodemus. He challenged them to reach beyond their limited way of thinking to embrace what could only be accessed by choosing to believe in Him.

Jesus answered, "The work of God is this: to believe in the one he has sent." (John 6:29)

Here is the gift for you to unwrap—it is a gift that needs to be unwrapped daily: *The Bread of Life.*

Just as your physical body awakens in the morning dependent on food—so your spiritual (real) body awakens in the morning dependent on spiritual food. Jesus is your bread of life.

Consider what God's Word says about spiritual bread:
He humbled you, causing you to hunger and then feeding you with manna, which neither you nor your fathers had

known, to teach you that man does not live by bread alone but on every word that comes from the mouth of the Lord. (Deuteronomy 8:3)

After fasting forty days and nights, he was hungry. The tempter came to him and said, "If you are the Son of God, tell these stones to become bread." Jesus answered, "Man does not live on bread alone but by every word that comes from the mouth of God." (Matthew 4:2-4)

Give us today our daily bread. (Matthew 6:11)

While they were eating, Jesus took bread, gave thanks and broke it, and gave it to his disciples, saying, "Take and eat; this is my body." (Matthew 26:26)

Jesus is the bread of life. He came from heaven to give us life. His life nourishes and sustains our own. Today and every day unwrap this incredible gift. Feast on the Bread of Life which is the Word of God. While bread made from wheat nourishes your physical body, so God's Word nourishes your eternal soul. The day will come when your body no longer eats—and soon thereafter you will be in the presence of God feasting on what this world's bread merely represented…the Bread of Life.

Perhaps that which seems real is really the shadow—and that which seems the shadow is really real.

UNWRAP THE GIFT OF HIS PRESENCE...

1. How might you feast on the "bread of life"?

2. How can you give your family "real" gifts this Christmas? Last year Tom and I gave each of our children a verbal blessing. We told them how proud we were of them and reminded them of specific situations in the previous year where we'd seen their character shine. Then we told them of how we anticipated their success in the new year. Oh, there were tears and blubbering, and I'm sure a little too much emotion for their comfort—but the "blessing" was most likely the gift they most remember. Although we couldn't wrap it with a bow—it was real.

PRAY THIS PRAYER: *Father, thank You for being the Bread of Life. Thank You that You are all sufficient to meet my spiritual needs. Thank You for providing me with all I need for life. I trust You. Please give me a spiritual hunger that is satisfied in You—just as my physical hunger is satisfied by food. In Jesus' name I pray. Amen*

CHAPTER 56

ORIGIN OF CHRISTMAS LIGHTS

In him was life, and that life was the light of men.
The light shines in the darkness,
but the darkness has not understood it.

John 1:4-5

I love Christmas lights. When my children were young-
er, I would pop popcorn and fill their little thermoses
with hot chocolate, pack them in the car, and we'd
travel all over Williamson County to see the lights. It was
a fun outing. Much to their chagrin, we never hung (and
still don't hang) Christmas lights on our own house. Our
lives are so hectic this time of the year, and Tom finds
more delight in hiding from ducks than he does climb-
ing up ladders—we simply hang two bows on the lights
that are already out there and put a wreath on the door.
Then, we enjoy the show our neighbors put on. One year
a friend of ours brought us a strand of lights and placed it
on a bush. She felt sorry for us and wanted to share some
of her Christmas lights with us.

I thought it would be fun to trace the origin of
Christmas lights and found this information from several
websites. Christmas lights originated in Germany when

wealthy families decorated their trees with candles. The candles were exchanged for lights when Edward Johnson used them on his tree. (Edward worked for none other than...Thomas Edison.) In the early 1900s the first strands of lights were sold by Ever Ready, then improved upon and sold by GE in the 1920s. Christmas lights were first placed on Christmas trees but gradually found their way outside homes, and today they even grace animated figures.

In Ireland people placed a candle in their window on Christmas Eve. This candle served as a beacon to those traveling who might need a place to stay. In memory of Joseph and Mary who had a hard time finding a place suitable to spend the night, the Irish hospitality extended to strangers with this candle in the window. It was an invitation to come inside.

Christmas lights symbolize the Christmas star—the one that led the wise men and heralded the birth of the King. The Christmas star symbolizes the moment when the Word became flesh and dwelt among us, shining His Light in the darkness. John mentions the light of the world in the very beginning of his gospel:

In the beginning was the Word, and the Word was with God, and the Word was God. He was with God in the beginning. Through him all things were made; without him nothing was made that has been made. In him was life, and that life was the light of men. The light shines in the darkness, but the darkness has not understood it. (John 1:1-5)

Jesus is the light of the world.

UNWRAP THE GIFT OF HIS PRESENCE...

1. What exactly does it mean that Jesus is the light of the world?

2. When it's dark tonight, turn on a light. Consider what that light does to your world.

PRAY THIS PRAYER: *Father of lights, shine down on me. Thank You for sending Jesus to be the light of the world. I so want to understand You and walk daily in Your light. Amen*

CHAPTER 57

LIGHT OF THE WORLD

Jesus declared, "I am the light of the world.
Whoever follows me will never walk in darkness,
but will have the light of life."

John 8:12

Often light is used in Scripture to represent knowledge and understanding. Consider these references to light in the Psalms:

The precepts of the Lord are right, giving joy to the heart. The commands of the Lord are radiant, giving light to the eyes. (Psalm 19:8)

The Lord is my light and my salvation—whom shall I fear? The Lord is the stronghold of my life—of whom shall I be afraid? (Psalm 27:1)

For you have delivered me from death and my feet from stumbling, that I may walk before God in the light of life. (Psalm 56:13)

He wraps himself in light as with a garment; he stretches out the heavens like a tent… (Psalm 104:2)

*Your word is a lamp to my feet and a light for my path.
(Psalm 119:105)*

*The unfolding of Your words gives light; it gives
understanding to the simple. (Psalm 119:130)*

The psalmists used *light* to represent understanding,
clarity, vision, and knowledge that God's presence had
been revealed. In contrast darkness was used to represent
confusion, lack of vision, foolishness, and God's absence.
When I was writing *Learning to Love Surrender*, I found
this in *Baker's Evangelical Dictionary of Biblical Theology*,

"Darkness and light are evocative words in Hebrew.
Darkness evokes everything that is anti-God: the
wicked (Prov 2:13), judgment (Ex 10:21), death
(Ps 88:12). Light is the first of the Creator's works,
manifesting the divine operation in a world that is
darkness and chaos without it. While light is not
itself divine, it is often used metaphorically for life
Ps 56:13), salvation (Isa 9:2), the commandments
(Prov 6:23), and the divine presence of God (Exodus
10:23)."

The light that God creates brings order to chaos.
When God sheds light into your life, He provides direction, hope, protection, and awareness of His presence.

And God said, "Let there be light," and there was light. God saw that the light was good, and he separated the light from the darkness." (Genesis 1:3-4)

UNWRAP THE GIFT OF HIS PRESENCE...

1. How has God's light brought order to chaos in your life?

2. In which areas of your life do you need Him to shine His light?

PRAY THIS PRAYER: *Lord, You have delivered me from death and my feet from stumbling that I may walk before You in the light of life (Psalm 56:3) Amen*

CHAPTER 58

THE LIGHT OF LIFE

I am the light of the world.
Whoever follows me will never walk in darkness,
but will have the light of life.

John 8:12

In the fullness of time, God brought Light Himself into the darkness! And when Jesus grew to be a man, He said this to Nicodemus,

"This is the verdict: Light has come into the world, but men loved darkness instead of light because their deeds were evil. Everyone who does evil hates the light, and will not come into the light for fear that his deeds will be exposed. But whoever lives by the truth comes into the light, so that it may be seen plainly that what he has done has been done through God." (John 3:19-21)

Then in John 8:12 Jesus declared, "I am the light of the world. Whoever follows me will never walk in darkness, but will have the light of life."

According to Neil Anderson, theologians have identified three means of divine revelation: general revelation, special revelation, and ultimate revelation.

Anderson writes, "General revelation is what can be observed and studied in nature. Psalm 19:1 reads, 'The heavens are telling of the glory of God; and their expanse is declaring the work of His hands.' Romans 1:20 says, 'For since the creation of the world His invisible attributes, His eternal power and divine nature, have been clearly seen.'"

Then he goes on to say, "Special revelation refers to the written Word of God. Protestants limit special revelation to the 66 canonical books divided into the Old Testament (39 books) and the New Testament (27 books)."

But ultimate revelation is the Person of Jesus Christ. "Jesus alone perfectly reveals who God is because He is God." (pp. 23-24 *Discipleship Counseling*, Regal Books, 2003) If light represented the presence of God as the psalmist wrote in the Old Testament, then Jesus truly is the ultimate revelation of God in the world today. He is the light of the world.

UNWRAP THE GIFT OF HIS PRESENCE...

1. How does the ultimate revelation of God in His Son Jesus affect the light in your world?

2. When I was a child, my father led us in lighting the advent candles at Christmas time. While dinners together are rare in my family of teens, they are still special. Consider lighting advent candles at your dinner tables this holiday season.

PRAY THIS PRAYER: *Lord, thank You for revealing Yourself to me—through nature, through Your Word, and especially through the Person of Jesus. Please shine Your life into [names of family members and friends who desperately need Jesus]. Help me to shine the light of Your love today. Amen*

CHAPTER 59

SHEEP IN SCRIPTURE

The Lord is my shepherd, I shall not want.
Psalm 23:1

When our children were in elementary school (well, if the truth be known, we continued to do this when they were in middle school too), we put on a play each Christmas Eve for my parents and sisters. The inspiration for this impromptu performance began the year Halo joined our family. Halo is our malti-poo. Mikel was six, and she only wanted one thing from Santa that year (this was the same year Mikel discovered the truth about Santa—but that is another story, one I will include in a bit). She wanted a little yellow puppy. After consulting with us, Santa decided a puppy was exactly what she needed, and he delivered her yellow puppy on the Saturday before Christmas.

We bundled "Halo" up and took him with us to Georgia for the holidays. (Halo makes this journey every Christmas—this will be his 10th!) He was so sweet, and Mikel was so happy we decided we had to do a play. So, Mikel dressed up like a shepherd, TJ was Joseph, and Kaleigh was Mary. Her baby doll served as the baby Jesus, and Halo was our token sheep. After that year we put on all kinds of performances: the Grinch, a Christmas Carol, and the 12 Days of Christmas…I can't even remember all the performances we did.

Isn't it great that sheep are part of the Christmas story? Other than John 3:16 and the Lord's prayer, perhaps the most quoted passage of Scripture is Psalm 23.

The Lord is my shepherd, I shall not want. He makes me lie down in green pastures, he leads me beside still waters, he restores my soul. He guides me in paths of righteousness for his name's sake. Even though I walk through the valley of the shadow of death, I will fear no evil, for you are with me; your rod and your staff, they comfort me. You prepare a table before me in the presence of my enemies. You anoint my head with oil; my cup overflows. Surely goodness and love will follow me all the days of my life, and I will dwell in the house of the Lord forever. (v.1-6)

Scripture relates people to sheep in more places than this Psalm. Isaiah 53:6 says,

We all, like sheep, have gone astray, each of us has turned to his own way; and the Lord has laid on him the iniquity of us all.

Jesus made reference to Himself as both the gate and the good Shepherd for his sheep:

Therefore Jesus said again, "I tell you the truth, I am the gate for the sheep. All who ever came before me were thieves

and robbers, but the sheep did not listen to them. I am the gate; whoever enters through me will be saved. He will come in and go out, and find pasture. The thief comes only to steal and kill and destroy; I have come that they may have life, and have it to the full.

I am the good shepherd. The good shepherd lays down his life for the sheep. The hired hand is not the shepherd who owns the sheep. So when he sees the wolf coming, he abandons the sheep and runs away. Then the wolf attacks the flock and scatters it. The man runs away because he is a hired hand and cares nothing for the sheep. I am the good shepherd; I know my sheep and my sheep know me—just as the Father knows me and I know the Father—and I lay down my life for the sheep." (John 10:7-15)

UNWRAP THE GIFT OF HIS PRESENCE...

1. What comes to your mind when you think of sheep?

2. Why would Jesus refer to Himself as the "gate for the sheep"?

3. What does He mean when He calls Himself the "good shepherd"?

PRAY THIS PRAYER: *Lord, when I think about those shepherds keeping watch over their flocks that night, I'm mindful that You think of me as sheep—a little lamb in desperate need of a shepherd. Thank You for loving me enough to tenderly lead me on. Amen*

CHAPTER 60

THE GATE FOR THE SHEEP

Therefore Jesus said again, "I tell you the truth,
I am the gate for the sheep. All who ever came before me
were thieves and robbers, but the sheep did not listen to
them. I am the gate; whoever enters through me will be
saved. He will come in and go out, and find pasture.
The thief comes only to steal and kill and destroy; I have
come that they may have life, and have it to the full."
John 10:7-10

Philip Keller, the professional sheep rancher from east Africa and author of *A Shepherd Looks at Psalm 23*, tells this story about this passage of Scripture.

"As winter, with its cold rains and chilling winds came on, my neighbor's sickly sheep would stand huddled at the fence, their tails to the storm facing the rich fields in which my flock flourished. Those poor abused, neglected creatures under the owner-ship of a heartless rancher had known nothing but suffering most of the year....some were so weak and thin and wretched that their thin legs could scarcely bear their scanty frames.

Always there seemed to lurk in their eyes the

slender, faint hope that perhaps with a bit of luck they could break through the fence or crawl through some hole to free themselves. Occasionally this used to happen, especially around Christmas. This was the time of extreme tides when the sea retreated far out beyond the end of the fence lines which ran down to it. The neighbor's emaciated, dissatisfied, hungry sheep would wait for this to happen. Then at the first chance they would go down on the tidal flats, slip around the end of the fence, and come sneaking in to gorge themselves on our rich green grass.

So pitiful and pathetic was their condition that the sudden feast of lush feed, to which they were unaccustomed, often proved disastrous... I clearly recall coming across three of my neighbor's ewes lying helpless under a fir tree near the fence one drizzly day. They were like three old, limp, gray, sodden sacks collapsed in a heap...I loaded them into a wheelbarrow and wheeled them back to their heartless owner. He simply pulled out a sharp killing knife and slit all three of their throats. He couldn't care less.

What a picture of Satan who holds ownership over so many.

Right there the graphic account Jesus portrayed of Himself as being the door and entrance by which sheep were to enter His fold flashed across my mind. Those poor sheep had not come into my land through the proper gate. I had never let them in. They had never really become mine…If they had, they would not have suffered so. Even starting out under my management they would have been given special care.

In short, they tried to get in on their own. It simply spelled disaster. What made it doubly sad was that they were doomed anyway. On the old impoverished ranch they would have starved to death that winter.

Likewise with those apart from Christ. The old world is a pretty wretched land, and Satan is a heartless owner. He cares not a whit for men's souls or welfare. Under his tyranny there are hundreds of hungry, discontented hearts who long to enter into the household of God—who ache for His care and concern.

Yet there is only one way into this fold. That way is through the owner, Christ himself—the Gate for His sheep." (pp. 168-170, *A Shepherd Looks at Psalm 23*, Zondervan, 2007)

Unwrap the gift of His presence...

1. Underline John 10:7-10 in your copy of God's Word.

2. What does the thief come to do to the sheep? How does the thief get in?

PRAY THIS PRAYER: *Thank You, Lord, for sending Jesus to make a way for me. Thank You for providing me protection in Your fold. Help me to be aware of the thief's intent and of his sneaky methods. Protect me and all my family so that we can point to You as our Good Shepherd. Amen*

CHAPTER 61

THE GOOD SHEPHERD IS PRESENT

*I am the good shepherd. The good shepherd lays down his life
for the sheep. The hired hand is not the shepherd who owns
the sheep. So when he sees the wolf coming, he abandons
the sheep and runs away. Then the wolf attacks the flock
and scatters it. The man runs away because he is
a hired hand and cares nothing for the sheep. I am the good
shepherd; I know my sheep and my sheep know me—
just as the Father knows me and I know the Father—
and I lay down my life for the sheep.*

John 10:11-15

It is a well-known fact that sheep are ignorant creatures. They desperately need a shepherd to save them
both from predators and from their own ignorance.
Keller says that for sheep to *lie down in green pastures* they
have to be free from fear, tension, aggravation, and hunger. Through his own experience, he discovered that his
sheep were most willing to rest when his presence was
with them. This is what he wrote, "In the course of time,
I came to realize that nothing so quieted and reassured
the sheep as to see me in the field. The presence of their
master and owner and protector put them at ease as noth-

209 · UNWRAP THE GIFT OF HIS PRESENCE

ing else could do, and this applied day and night." (Philip Keller, *A Shepherd Looks at Psalm 23*, p. 44, Zondervan, 2007)

When Jesus said, "I am the good shepherd," He assured us that His presence was enough. His presence IS enough. When Jesus is present, all is well. Circumstances might be unimaginably difficult—but, God is on His throne, and that is enough.

I was walking toward the graveside of a young husband and father. His wife was shaken by the cancer that defeated him. Tom walked by her side, and I followed behind. I never even thought about the fact that Tom was comforting the new widow as I walked alone behind the others. My head was down and my heart low when I felt the slightest touch of a hand grabbing my fingers. I looked up and into the eyes of my husband. For just a moment we shared an intimate moment in the inexpressible place of grief.

There is a ministry of presence that far exceeds any other. God knew that our deepest need was to have Him present in our lives. That's why He sent Immanuel—which means, "God with us."

UNWRAP THE GIFT OF HIS PRESENCE...

1. Underline Isaiah 7:14 in your copy of God's Word.

2. Reflect on the significance of God's powerful personal presence in your life.

PRAY THIS PRAYER: *Lord, thank You for being my good Shepherd—for promising to stay with me no matter what. I want to learn to hear Your voice so that I can follow You wherever You may go. Amen*

CHAPTER 62

GREEN PASTURES

The LORD is my shepherd, I shall not want.
He makes me lie down in green pastures;
He leads me beside quiet waters.
Psalm 23:1-2 NASB

When I was young, I read Psalm 23:1 and thought that David was saying that the Lord was his shepherd that he did not want! It was an "ah ha" moment in my life when I realized that he was saying, "The Lord is my shepherd, therefore I will not want for anything else."

Jesus said He was a "good shepherd." Part of being a good shepherd is not only remaining present with the sheep but also getting sheep to *lie down in green pastures.* The good shepherd knows where these pastures are—and he leads his sheep to them. Philip Keller wrote,

"A hungry ill-fed sheep is ever on its feet, on the move, searching for another scanty mouthful of forage to try and satisfy its gnawing hunger. Such sheep are not contented, they do not thrive, they are of no use to themselves nor to their owners. They languish and lack vigor and vitality.

In the Scriptures the picture portrayed of the Promised Land, to which God tried so hard to lead Israel from Egypt, was that of a 'land flowing with milk and honey.' Not only is this figurative language but also essentially scientific terminology. In agricultural terms we speak of a 'milk flow' and 'honey flow.' By this we mean the peak season of productive stages. The livestock that feed on forage and the bees that visit the blossoms are said to be producing a corresponding 'flow' of milk and honey. So a land flowing with milk and honey is a land of rich, green, luxuriant pastures.

And when God spoke of such a land for Israel He also foresaw such an abundant life of joy and victory and contentment for His people.

For the child of God, the Old Testament account of Israel moving from Egypt into the Promised Land is a picture of us moving from sin into the life of overcoming victory. We are promised such a life. It has been provided for us and is made possible by the unrelenting effort of Christ on our behalf." (pp. 54-55)

When Jesus said, "I am the good shepherd," He knew that He intended to pave the way to green pastures—a land that is flowing with milk and honey. When we yield ourselves to the lordship of Christ—when we allow Him to till the soil of our minds and heart (by removing unbelief, bitterness, pride, and self-sufficiency) we enter in to the life He died to give us.

"I am the good shepherd; I know my sheep and my sheep know me just as the Father knows me and I know the Father—and I lay down my life for the sheep." (John 10:14-15)

UNWRAP THE GIFT OF HIS PRESENCE—

1. Read Psalm 23 aloud. Reflect on the goodness of your Shepherd.

2. When you place the sheep in your nativity scene, ask God to bring to mind family and friends who are still outside the fold. Pray for these by name and invite the Lord to give you an opportunity to share with them this holiday season.

PRAY THIS PRAYER: *Father, thank You for sending Jesus to be the gate for the sheep. Thank You for calling me by name. Thank You for offering me peace, security, and rest. I trust You—my good Shepherd. Amen*

CHAPTER 63

WRAPPED IN
SWADDLING CLOTHES

*While they were there, the time came for the baby
to be born, and she gave birth to her firstborn, a son.
She wrapped him in cloths and placed him in a manger…*
Luke 2:6-7

*This will be a sign to you: You will find a baby
wrapped in cloths and lying in a manger.*
Luke 2:12

I have always loved the thought of the Son of Man wrapped in swaddling clothes. If you are a mother, and you gave birth to your child(ren), remember how they wrapped them and placed them in the plastic buckets? Those little blankets tucked tightly around those tiny little bodies, and held them snug as a bug in a rug. Jesus was wrapped in swaddling clothes, just as our newborn babies are wrapped today.

As you wrap your Christmas gifts, think of those swaddling clothes. He might not have had a bow, but Jesus was nonetheless wrapped—our tiny, perfect Christmas present.

Now consider what the women found when they

went to His tomb on Easter morning. Here is an excerpt from my book *Women Touched by Jesus*. This is how the women might have reported what they experienced:

"We got up early. We'd decided to do this because we hadn't had time to properly prepare His body for burial because of the Sabbath laws and all. Mary gathered the frankincense, I took the myrrh. On the way there, we wondered how we'd get the stone moved out of the way. But as soon as we arrived, Joanna (you know Jo, she always has to rush ahead! Why, just the other day, [deep sigh] never mind.) Joanna yelled back to us, 'the stone! It's rolled away!' She waited until we got there to walk on in. I was trembling as we approached the slab where they'd laid his body. He was not there! I mean it, bless His sweet heart. He was gone! His grave clothes were folded neatly at the foot of the slab as if He'd taken His time to tidy up before He left! Mary, Joanna and I fell to our knees. We were frightened and excited all at the same time!

Suddenly two marvelous creatures stood before us. They were *like* men but seemed to glow with light! Their robes were pure white! I've never been able to get anything that clean. (I scrub, rinse, scrub… how do you deal with stain? I'm so sorry; I got off the subject again.) Anyway, these men…these heavenly messengers asked us, 'Why are you looking for the living among the dead? He is not here! He's risen just as He said!'"

I wrote this to demonstrate the difference in how men might tell the resurrection story as compared to how women might tell it (and make my point that God knew what He was doing when He assigned the task to women). But all fun aside, don't you find it interesting that at Christmas our gift is wrapped and at Easter He's unwrapped?

Isn't that the wonder of it all?! Jesus—the perfect gift came to us wrapped (in swaddling clothes) and then came back to us unwrapped (leaving His grave clothes behind). Consider your Christmas presents. While they look pretty and decorate the tree, the real joy of the gift is not the package wrapped, but the gift unwrapped! I thank God that He completed the work He began in Jesus, and that He unwrapped for us eternal life.

UNWRAP THE GIFT OF HIS PRESENCE...

1. When you wrap your gifts this year, think of those swaddling clothes Mary wrapped around her newborn babe.

2. When you unwrap your gifts with family and friends, share the message of today's devotion—remind them of the gift "unwrapped" that came to us on Easter morning.

PRAY THIS PRAYER: *Father, thank You for the gift of life that begins the moment we unwrap the gift of Your Son through confessing with our mouths, "Jesus is Lord" and believing in our hearts You raised Him from the dead. Continue to reveal to me the resurrection power that is mine. Amen*

CHAPTER 64

LAZARUS AND GOD'S GLORY

When he heard this, Jesus said, "This sickness will not end in death. No, it is for God's glory so that God's Son may be glorified through it." Jesus loved Martha and her sister and Lazarus. Yet when he heard that Lazarus was sick, he stayed where he was two more days.

John 11:4-6

Jesus is the resurrection and the life. He demonstrated this truth when He raised Lazarus from the dead. This miracle is recorded in John 11. I love how John stated the fact that Jesus loved Martha, her sister, and Lazarus, and yet He stayed where He was and didn't come to their rescue when they called Him. Don't ever forget that God's silence is not an indicator of His lack of love. He loves you and that is a fact no matter how quickly He responds to your desperate cries for help.

When Jesus finally did go to Lazarus' home, Lazarus had been in the tomb for four days. Understandably Martha greeted Jesus in this way,

"Lord, … if you had been here, my brother would not have died." (John 11:21)

What a powerful declaration of her faith. And this would have been enough—but she went on to say,

"But I know that even now God will give you whatever you ask." (John 11:22)

Martha knew Jesus well. In response to her faith, Jesus said,

"Your brother will rise again."

Martha answered, "I know he will rise again in the resurrection at the last day."

Jesus said to her, "I am the resurrection and the life. He who believes in me will live, even though he dies; and whoever live and believes in me will never die. Do you believe this?" (John 11:23-26)

Because Martha had spent many hours with Jesus, she believed He was the Son of God. So all that He was telling her was truth she had already embraced.

"Yes, Lord," she told him, "I believe that you are the Christ, the Son of God, who was to come into the world." (John 11:27)

However, Martha's belief in Jesus' everlasting life was limited to what happened on the other side of the grave. Her personal experience was that death still delivered the final blow—and her brother had died, only to rise to eternal (not physical) life. We know this because of how Martha responded to Jesus' request that they remove the stone from the entrance to Lazarus' tomb.

Jesus, once more deeply moved, came to the tomb. It was a cave with a stone laid across the entrance. "Take away the stone," he said. "But, Lord," said Martha, the sister of the

dead man, "*by this time there is a bad odor, for he has been there four days.*"

Then Jesus said, "*Did I not tell you that if you believed, you would see the glory of God?*"

So they took away the stone. Then Jesus looked up and said, "*Father, I thank you that you have heard me. I knew that you always hear me, but I said this for the benefit of the people standing here, that they may believe that you sent me.*"

When he had said this, Jesus called in a loud voice, "*Lazarus, come out!*" The dead man came out, his hands and feet wrapped with strips of linen, and a cloth around his face. Jesus said to them, "*Take off the grave clothes and let him go.*" (John 11:38-44)

There's another gift unwrapped.

UNWRAP THE GIFT OF HIS PRESENCE...

1. Can you imagine Martha's wonder and joy?

2. How do you think Lazarus' return from the dead might have rocked Martha's world?

PRAY THIS PRAYER: *Lord, help me to trust You more—to take You at Your Word and eagerly anticipate moments that will take my breath away. Amen*

CHAPTER 65

RESURRECTION POWER

*Jesus said to her, "Your brother will rise again." Martha
answered, "I know he will rise again in the resurrection at
the last day." Jesus said to her, "I am the resurrection and
the life. He who believes in Me will live, even though he dies;
and whoever lives and believes in me will never die.
Do you believe this?" "Yes, Lord," she told him,
"I believe that you are the Christ, the Son of God,
who was to come into the world."*

John 11:23-27

I have always related well to Martha. I am a take-charge kind of girl. I have no problem leading, and I am much more likely to rush around preparing dinners than I am to be sitting at Jesus' feet. Also like Martha, I trust Jesus. If I'd been in her sandals, I too would have run out to greet Jesus and assured Him of my confidence in Him even though He didn't come when I called. But also like Martha, I tend to relegate the power of the resurrection to something I am only going to experience when I leave this earthly tent and make the mysterious journey to heaven when I die.

But this story in John 11 and several challenges that Paul presented to the early church in his epistles have caused me to wonder, is there more to the resurrection than life on the other side of the grave? Is there resurrection power that gives purpose, meaning, and victory to my life while I'm still living here below? If so, I don't want to miss the full truth of Jesus' resurrection power!

Consider what Paul wrote to the Ephesians:

I pray also that the eyes of your heart may be enlightened in order that you may know the hope to which he has called you, the riches of his glorious inheritance in the saints, and his incomparably great power for us who believe. That power is like the working of his mighty strength, which he exerted in Christ when he raised him from the dead and seated him at his right hand in the heavenly realms. (Ephesians 1:18-20)

When Jesus proclaimed Himself the Resurrection and the Life, He meant here and now, as well as then and there. Don't stay all swaddled in the tight clothes of what the world says about the natural order of things. Take God at His Word, and unwrap the marvelous gift of resurrection power and eternal life.

UNWRAP THE GIFT OF HIS PRESENCE . . .

1. Have you ever experienced God do the impossible in your life? If so, when? Celebrate the resurrection power that is working like mighty strength in your world today.

2. What are you wanting God's resurrection power to do in or through you today?

PRAY THIS PRAYER: *Lord, open the eyes of my heart so that I might become more aware of the hope that You have for me. Let me experience Your incomparably great power—the same power that raised Jesus from the dead and seated Him at Your right hand in the heavenly realms. Amen*

CHAPTER 66

THE VINE

I am the true vine, and my Father is the gardener. He cuts
off every branch that does not bear fruit, while every branch
that does bear fruit he prunes so that it will be even more
fruitful. You are already clean because of the word I have
spoken to you. Remain in me, and I will remain in you.
No branch can bear fruit by itself; it must remain in the
vine. Neither can you bear fruit unless you remain in me.
I am the vine; you are the branches. If a man remains in
me and I in him, he will bear much fruit;
apart from me you can do nothing.

John 15:1-5

J esus taught using commonplace illustrations. Vine-
yards were tended perhaps just over the hill from
where Jesus might have stood when He voiced the
words in John 15. Seeing the vines, Jesus simply stated, "I
am the true vine…"

Too many people think they have to work for God.
Some embrace a martyr's complex carrying the burden of
lostness, missions education, worship, leadership devel-
opment, outreach, special needs; the list could go on and
on. They think that God will somehow be handicapped
if they don't "get it done"!

Don't forget that the Enemy's chief strategy is deception. He creates deception by making the counterfeit look like the authentic. I wonder how many churches think they are about their Father's business. The work they do produces activity, perhaps it even generates growth—but because they accomplish it in their own strength apart from Christ, it amounts to *nothing*.

When Jesus said, "*I am the vine*," He explained that God's work is produced through us when we are *abiding* or *remaining* in Him. For "no branch can bear fruit by itself; it must remain in the vine. Neither can you bear fruit unless you remain in me."

One of the best illustrations of this truth is found in Luke 10:38-42. In this brief snapshot into Jesus' personal life we discover that Mary sat at Jesus' feet and listened to His words while Martha was "distracted with all her preparations." Out of anger and indignation Martha asked Jesus to tell Mary to help her. But much to Martha's surprise, Jesus rebuked her instead of Mary with this powerful statement,

But the Lord answered and said to her, "Martha, Martha, you are worried and bothered about so many things; but only one thing is necessary, for Mary has chosen the good part, which shall not be taken away from her." (Luke 10:41-42 NASB)

He is the vine; we are the branches. Don't get distracted and miss abiding in Him.

Unwrap the gift of His presence...

1. How have you been guilty of working for Jesus rather than allowing Him to work through you?

2. What will you do differently today?

Pray this prayer: *Lord, I don't want to be distracted by so many things. Help me to sit at Your feet long enough to listen to Your words. Help me to trust You when my plate is too full, and You ask me to scrape some off. Show me what needs to be let go today. Amen*

CHAPTER 67

ABIDE IN HIM

*I am the vine, you are the branches; he who abides in Me
and I in him, he bears much fruit, for apart from Me you
can do nothing. If anyone does not abide in Me,
he is thrown away as a branch and dries up; and they gather
them, and cast them into the fire and they are burned.
If you abide in Me, and My words abide in you, ask
whatever you wish, and it will be done for you. My Father is
glorified by this, that you bear much fruit, and so prove to be
My disciples. Just as the Father has loved Me,
I have also loved you; abide in My love. If you keep My
commandments, you will abide in My love; just as I have
kept My Father's commandments and abide in His love.
These things I have spoken to you so that My joy may be
in you, and that your joy may be made full.*

John 15:5-11 NASB

When Tom and I started working with our church (the 8 people that made up our congregation), we put into practice all that we learned in seminary. But after seven years of steady growth (that included strong programs and solid biblical teaching), we came face to face with obstacles we had never encountered before. People grew suspicious and disgruntled. Some held "secret" meetings in their homes—and others whispered in the hallways of the church. I'll never forget the afternoon that Tom came home from church, plopped down in his favorite chair, and said, "Leighann, they may fire me tonight. But it's going to be OK."

I think it was at that moment that he and I truly understood what John 15:5 meant. We realized with a certainty that came from being enrolled in the school of hard knocks that "apart from Christ we could do nothing." All the good things we knew to do, all the great things we were taught to do, all the things that brought great results in the first seven years of our ministry as our church grew from 8 to 280, were being torn apart by dissension. And even though we were in essence the "founding pastors" of this church, we were "done for" apart from God's intervention.

As we sat together at the next business meeting and tried to make sense out of what seemed to be crumbling around us, we clung to the Vine. I wish I could tell you that on that very night the Holy Spirit miraculously swept through our service and brought unity. But He didn't. Tom suffered more accusations, and people left the meeting frustrated and angry. For several more months we clung to our Vine, trusting that whatever fruit He had in mind to produce through us would have to come only from our abiding, for we were clinging to Him so desperately we didn't have much energy for anything else.

That was 15 years ago. Since then our church has grown from 280 to over 2,000. In our 21+ years at this church we've witnessed marriages restored, souls saved, babies born, cancer destroyed, prodigals return home—God has produced abundant fruit through us. And I say that with the utmost humility. For all Tom and I have done is cling to the Vine.

If you will abide in Him, He will abide in you. And you will discover that although the work is exhausting, the results are amazing. You will also discover that God never called you to produce fruit—only to abide. God is the fruit-producer; you are merely the vine-abider.

UNWRAP THE GIFT OF HIS PRESENCE...

1. Underline John 15:5 in your copy of God's Word.

2. Can you think of a time when you learned the difference between working *for* God and allowing God to accomplish His work *through* you?

PRAY THIS PRAYER: *Father, I confess that often I try to do Your work for You. I confess that my pride makes me think that I can do what only You can do. Please forgive me for this pride. I am choosing right now to abide in You—and to trust You to bear Your fruit through me. Thank You for allowing Jesus to be the Vine. I am perfectly content being a branch. In Jesus' name I pray. Amen*

CHAPTER 68

THE HOLY SPIRIT

*But I tell you the truth: It is for your good that I am going
away. Unless I go away, the Counselor will not come to
you; but if I go, I will send him to you. When he comes, he
will convict the world of guilt in regard to sin, because men
do not believe in me; in regard to righteousness, because
I am going to the Father, where you can see me no longer;
and in regard to judgment, because the prince of this world
now stands condemned. I have much more to say to you,
more than you can now bear. But when he, the Spirit of
truth, comes, he will guide you into all truth. He will not
speak on his own; he will speak only what he hears,
and he will tell you what is yet to come. He will bring glory
to me by taking from what is mine and making it known
to you. All that belongs to the Father is mine.
That is why I said the Spirit will take from what is mine
and make it known to you.*

John 16:7-15

When I was a child, Casper "the friendly ghost" was a popular cartoon. He floated around with some other ghostly characters and got into trouble, but it was all in great fun. Perhaps the creators of Casper wanted to take the edge off the scariness of ghosts. But because I heard God's Spirit called the *Holy Ghost*, for many years I pictured Him resembling Casper. How tragic! For God's Holy Spirit does not in the least bit even slightly resemble Casper the friendly ghost.

The Holy Spirit is the Living Spirit of the living God! He was with God in the beginning; He participated in the creation just as Jesus did. When God breathed into man the "breath of life," the Spirit was in that breath. Sin dismissed the Spirit of God from Adam and Eve. But Jesus came to bring Him back. When Scripture speaks of the Holy Spirit, it speaks of the most holy, highest power in the universe. The Holy Spirit is the Creator and Sustainer of life. And Christ gave Him to us.

God gave us Jesus, and on Christmas Day we celebrate His birth. But Jesus didn't stay on earth. His earthly existence ended when He was around 33 years old. I often wish I could have lived during the 33 years that Jesus walked on the earth. I would have liked to have seen Him. I would have enjoyed hearing Him speak. I like to imagine what it might have been like to touch His feet or to feel the warmth of His embrace. I told a friend of mine that although she was single, God could be a husband to her. She honestly responded, "Yes, but I sure would like a husband I could hold." I sometimes feel this way about Jesus. I wonder what it would have been like to rock Him in my arms—like Mary rocked Him. Or to sit at His feet like the other Mary sat. I wonder what it would have been like to share His joy—to tell Him a joke and listen to Him laugh. But Jesus said that the One who came in His place was better even than He.

> *But I tell you the truth: It is for your good that I am going away. Unless I go away, the Counselor will not come to you; but if I go, I will send him to you. When he comes, he will convict the world of guilt in regard to sin, because men do not believe in me; in regard to righteousness, because I am going to the Father, where you can see me no longer; and in regard to judgment, because the prince of this world now stands condemned.*
>
> *I have much more to say to you, more than you can now bear. But when he, the Spirit of truth, comes, he will guide you into all truth. He will not speak on his own; he will speak only what he hears, and he will tell you what is yet to come. He will bring glory to me by taking from what is mine and making it known to you. All that belongs to the Father is mine. That is why I said the Spirit will take from what is mine and make it known to you. (John 16:7-15)*

Jesus said that He was returning to His Father so that we could have the Holy Spirit.

UNWRAP THE GIFT OF HIS PRESENCE...

1. Why is it better for us to have the Holy Spirit with us instead of Jesus?

2. How do you think the disciples felt about this when Jesus told them they'd be better off without Him?

PRAY THIS PRAYER: *Father, thank You for being all wise and all knowing. If You say I am better off with Your Spirit than I am with the earthly, bodily presence of Jesus, then I will rest in the truth of Your Word. Open my mind and heart to be more aware of Your presence here with me. Help me to recognize and sense Your power and Your love. Amen*

CHAPTER 69

THE HOLY SPIRIT WORKS

*When he comes, he will convict the world of guilt
in regard to sin and righteousness and judgment…*
John 16:8

When I was in high school I ran on the track team. My favorite events were the relay races. Each person took a "leg" of the race. Each one did her part to win her "leg" of the race, but when her distance was completed, she passed the baton to the next runner.

Jesus' words to His disciples in this passage of Scripture remind me of this race. Jesus came to earth to pave our way to God. He brought us forgiveness of sin; He fed us the bread of life; He illuminated the darkness with His Presence and revealed to us the ultimate revelation of God. Jesus became our gateway to God and eternal life, He was the good Shepherd offering us the ultimate gift— the gift of His life. And when He rose from the dead, He proclaimed the powerful strength of God that raised Him from the dead, and extended victory over sin and death to each of His own. Jesus became the Vine…but when He left, He passed the baton to the Holy Spirit.

According to this passage in John 16, the Holy Spirit

convicts men of sin. What a glorious thing! Apart from the conviction of sin, there can be no salvation. He also convicts men of righteousness. The Holy Spirit points to God and to Jesus Christ and declares the stark contrast between light and darkness. The Holy Spirit also brings judgment to the prince of this world. When Jesus died on the cross, the penalty for sin was paid, the curse of death was broken. Man is no longer condemned to live in the valley of the shadow of death (this sin-stained and broken world). The power of accusation and shame that the prince of this world held over man was made null and void. The Holy Spirit reminds the prince of this world that he is defeated—that the condemnation that he flung on man now belongs solely to him. Judgment has come to the prince of darkness—the Holy Spirit executes this judgment and binds the Deceiver.

The Holy Spirit will guide you in all truth. He will light your way. Because the Enemy seeks to deceive you, the Holy Spirit will guide you out of his tricky deceptions. You will walk in truth as you yield your mind and your heart to the power of God's Word as revealed to you through the Holy Spirit. He will serve as a companion when you read and study. He will make God's Word personal, living, active, and penetrating. The Holy Spirit will guide you in truth—because the enemy will try to distract you with lies.

Unwrap the gift of His presence...

1. Think over the past few days—have you sensed any conviction of sin? Have you learned (or been reminded of) a powerful truth? If so, thank God for the precious gift of the Holy Spirit.

2. If you have children, consider purchasing the book *The Song of the King* by Max Lucado and reading it together as a family. I dare you to do this if you have teens!! It might be fun to discuss how "hope-nots" attack their lives today.

Pray this prayer: *Father, Thank You for sending the Holy Spirit. Thank You for guiding me in the truth. I long to walk in intimate companionship with You so that I will never mistake Your voice for another. Amen*

CHAPTER 70

PRAYER

Therefore, brothers, since we have confidence
to enter the Most Holy Place by the blood of Jesus,
by a new and living way opened for us through the curtain,
that is, his body, and since we have a great priest over
the house of God, let us draw near to God with a sincere
heart in full assurance of faith having our hearts sprinkled
to cleanse us from a guilty conscience and having
our bodies washed with pure water.
Let us hold unswervingly to the hope we profess,
for he who promised is faithful.
Hebrews 10:19-23

When God gave us His Son, He restored our ability to communicate directly with Him. Prior to Jesus' death on the cross, prayer was offered through sacrifice and priestly intercession. The holy of holies was off limits to the ordinary man. But through Jesus' death, God removed the veil. He took away the separation between His holiness and our sin. Through the blood of Jesus, God made atonement for our sin thus creating a way (the gate for the sheep) for us to enter His throne room boldly and cry out to Him the same intensity and intimacy that His Son cried. We can call out, "Abba, Father!" And know that when we do—He hears our voice.

Paul teaches this truth in Hebrews:

...but because Jesus lives forever, he has a permanent priesthood. Therefore he is able to save completely those who come to God through him, because he always lives to intercede for them. Such a high priest meets our needs—one who is holy, blameless, pure, set apart from sinners, exalted above the heavens. Unlike the other high priests, he does not need to offer sacrifices day after day, first for his own sins, and then for the sins of the people. He sacrificed for their sins once for all when he offered himself. (Hebrews 7:24-27)

Therefore, brothers, since we have confidence to enter the Most Holy Place by the blood of Jesus, by a new and living way opened for us through the curtain, that is, his body, and since we have a great priest over the house of God, let us draw near to God with a sincere heart in full assurance of faith having our hearts sprinkled to cleanse us from a guilty conscience and having our bodies washed with pure water. Let us hold unswervingly to the hope we profess, for he who promised is faithful. (Hebrews 10:19-23)

Unfortunately most children of God still fumble about in darkness because they don't know how to enter in to this holy place. They consider prayer boring, unnecessary, ineffective—or worse, they don't consider prayer at all. The Enemy has many believers living in the fog because he's convinced them that prayer doesn't matter.

UNWRAP THE GIFT OF HIS PRESENCE...

1. Why is prayer important?

2. What is the value of having full access to the throne room of God?

PRAY THIS PRAYER: *Lord, I know that You have many blessings in store for me as I learn to come boldly to Your throne. Please teach me to pray. Amen*

CHAPTER 71

PRAYER AND INTIMACY

*For this reason a man will leave his father and mother
and be united to his wife, and the two will become one flesh.
This is a profound mystery—but I am talking about Christ
and the church. However, each one of you also
must love his wife as he loves himself,
and the wife must respect her husband.*

Ephesians 5:31-33

I happen to be married, therefore I am thrilled to share with you my living illustration of this mystery—the mystery being the intimacy we can share with God through Christ.

For me, it all began in October of 1988. On Sunday night Tom and Bert came to see my roommate Georgia at 1009 James Ave., in Ft. Worth, Texas. Tom saw me instead. As fate would have it, Georgia received a long distance call from one of her brothers and took her leave from our visit. I was left to entertain Tom and Bert for her.

What followed was our first date. We were dirt poor (having come straight from college to graduate school) but didn't know it because we lived in a world where everyone was poor. On that first evening together, Tom took me to the Chinese Kitchen. It was a buffet style restaurant that used the same red trays you get at Arby's. We walked through our buffet line, chose our entrée, rice, egg roll and side dish, filled our Styrofoam cups with tea and sat down at a booth. The booth had seats that matched the red trays. After sprinkling soy sauce on our fried rice we began our conversation (or I began our conversation). Much to my chagrin, this outgoing, charismatic man was suddenly quiet. I started with my list of "questions to ask on the first date when your date doesn't talk."

1. Do you have any brothers or sisters? "Yes, three brothers."
2. What sports did you play growing up? "Football, basketball, baseball, and tennis. I played tennis in high school and college when I decided I was too small for football."
3. When did you start life guarding? "When I was 15."
4. Why did you come to seminary? "Because I think God is calling me to be an evangelist."
5. Why did you choose Southwestern? "Because my best friend Jamie came here."
6. Tell me about becoming a Christian? "I first asked Jesus into my heart when I was seven, but was baptized again in college after my friend Jamie challenged me to have a quiet time for a year."

With his brief answers and my list of questions exhausted, my chicken chow mein expanded and my swallower retracted. I prayed to survive this uncomfortable date until we got to the dollar theater where our action hero could take over the conversation.

Do you remember your first dates? What a mess!! Then came the turmoil between dates:

♦ What if he doesn't call, what if he does?
♦ What's he thinking?
♦ Does he like me?
♦ Do I like him?
♦ And the most difficult of all—if he does call, and you do want him to if he does like you and you like him, and he actually asks you out on another date…What should I wear?

UNWRAP THE GIFT OF HIS PRESENCE…

1. Remember the apprehension, the fear…the uncertainty? Does your prayer life resemble that first date feeling?

2. If so, how might you overcome that?

PRAY THIS PRAYER: *Lord, teach me to pray. Amen*

CHAPTER 72

JESUS PRAYED FOR HIS DISCIPLES

I have revealed you to those whom you gave me out of the world. They were yours; you gave them to me and they have obeyed your word. Now they know that everything you have given me comes from you. For I gave them the words you gave me and they accepted them. They know with certainty that I came from you, and they believed that you sent me. I pray for them. I am not praying for the world, but for those you have given me, for they are yours.

John 17:6-9

God sent Jesus to earth because He loves you and desires intimacy with you. This truth is best described in John 17. In this chapter, we get to eavesdrop on Jesus' prayer life. Most of the prayers that Jesus prayed while He was walking on the earth were off limits to His disciples. But in this particularly intimate prayer time, His disciples were invited to listen as Jesus poured His heart out to His Father.

The background of this passage of Scripture is this: Jesus was preparing His disciples for His coming death. They understood many things, but a major storm—crisis—was approaching. Jesus knew that during this crisis everything He'd been telling them about victory and His coming kingdom would be challenged. Jesus also knew that His death was approaching, and just as any friend—or even parent might do—He interceded on behalf of those He loved that would be left behind.

First Jesus prayed for Himself (John 17:1-5). Then He prayed for His disciples in John 17:6-9.

As Jesus directed His prayer toward His disciples, He gave His Father the report in more detail. Notice Jesus revealed God "to those whom You gave me" (v. 6). How could Jesus be so sure He'd chosen the right disciples? The answer is found in Luke.

One of those days Jesus went out to a mountainside to pray, and spent the night praying to God. When morning came, he called his disciples to him and chose twelve of them, whom he designated apostles: Simon (whom he named Peter), his brother Andrew, James, John, Philip, Bartholomew, Matthew, Thomas, James son of Alphaeus, Simon who was called the Zealot, Judas son of James, and Judas Iscariot, who became a traitor. (Luke 6:12-16)

Because Jesus prayed the entire night before He named His twelve disciples, He didn't wonder if He'd made the wrong decision when Peter denied Him. Jesus didn't feel defeated when Judas betrayed Him. He did not wring His hands in despair when James and John argued over the exalted positions in His Kingdom's government. Jesus didn't call a screeching halt to the crucifixion proceedings when every one of His followers deserted Him. Jesus knew these were God's chosen men for the job because He'd prayed all night for specific direction. Jesus' confidence in the future of His church was never based on the actions and attitudes of His disciples. Jesus confidence in the future of His church was and is based on the power and activity of the Holy Spirit.

UNWRAP THE GIFT OF HIS PRESENCE...

1. Don't miss this powerful truth. Jesus never had to second guess His decisions because He prayed before He made them! How might your life be different if you did the same?

2. Do you believe God will give you specific answers to specific prayers? Why or why not?

PRAY THIS PRAYER: *Lord, help me to understand the power of prayer. Help me to experience the same kind of intimacy great saints before me have experienced. Please speak to me in the details and specifics of my life. Amen*

CHAPTER 73

"I PRAY FOR THEM"

*I pray for them. I am not praying for the world,
but for those you have given me, for they are yours.*

John 17:9

Jesus made a request on behalf of His disciples: "*I pray for them. I am not praying for the world, but for those you have given me, for they are yours. All I have is yours, and all you have is mine. And glory has come to me through them. I will remain in the world no longer, but they are still in the world, and I am coming to you. Holy Father, protect them by the power of your name—the name you gave me—so that they may be one as we are one. While I was with them, I protected them and kept them safe by that name you gave me. None has been lost except the one doomed to destruction so that Scripture would be fulfilled.*

I am coming to you now, but I say these things while I am still in the world, so that they may have the full measure of my joy within them. I have given them your word and the world has hated them, for they are not of the world. My prayer is not that you take them out of the world but that you protect them from the evil one. They are not of the world, even as I am not of it. Sanctify them by the truth; your word is truth. As you sent me into the world, I have sent them into the world. For

them I sanctify myself, that they too may be truly sanctified."
(John 17:9-19)

One of the sweetest phrases in God's Word is in verse
9: "I pray for them." Jesus, God's Son...the One who
KNOWS us intimately...loves us PERFECTLY is ever in-
terceding on our behalf. Hebrews 7:25 says, *"He is able to
save completely those who come to God through Him, because
He always lives to intercede for them."*

You are reading this devotion because Jesus is inter-
ceding on your behalf. He's praying for you and me, right
now! In this passage, what seems to be Jesus' biggest concern? What is His heart cry?

*"My prayer is not that you take them out of the world but
that you protect them from the evil one."* (John 17:15)

Do you hear His heart? "I'm leaving them. I won't
be there to take care of them any longer. Now that I've
revealed truth to them, they are no longer of this world.
The world will hate them. Don't take them out of the
world, just protect them from the evil one!"

How does God protect us from the evil one? *"Sanctify
them by the truth; your word is truth."* (John 17:17)

Notice first that Jesus did not pray for the physical
safety of His disciples. He already knew (and even told
them) that they would be persecuted and that some of
them would suffer a martyr's death because of their faith
in Him. Jesus asked God for their spiritual protection.

God knows Satan is cunning and deceiving. He knows that Satan will try to breed doubt and despair into your prayer life. Remember the "patriot missiles" that intercepted the "scud" attacks in the early days of our war on terrorism? The best "patriot missile" you can use to render Satan's scud attacks powerless is God's Word. Immerse yourself in God's Word—which is truth. Memorize Scripture, and confess God's promises aloud when the enemy unleashes his scud attacks on you.

UNWRAP THE GIFT OF HIS PRESENCE...

1. How had God's Word protected you from the evil one?

2. Do you memorize Scripture? Consider making a commitment to memorize Scripture if you don't already. Consider challenging your family to memorize a verse a month.

PRAY THIS PRAYER: *Father, thank You again for sanctifying Your Son so that I could be truly sanctified. Reveal to me the full truth of my privileged position as one who is sanctified in Your presence. Allow the truth of Your Word concerning me to bear fruit of boldness and faith as I commit myself to You today. Amen*

CHAPTER 74

JESUS PRAYED FOR US

My prayer is not for them alone. I pray also for those
who will believe in me through their message, that all of them
may be one, Father, just as you are in me and I am in you.
May they also be in us so that the world may believe that you
have sent me. I have given them the glory that you gave me,
that they may be one as we are one: I in them
and you in me. May they be brought to complete unity
to let the world know that you sent me and have
loved them even as you have loved me.
John 17:20-23

As our study of John 17 continues, we finally come to the place where Jesus prayed for us. We find in these verses a perfect description of oneness with the Father. "I pray…that all of them may be one…just as you are in me and I am in you…" Remember the original order of things before the fall of man? In the original order, perfect unity existed between Adam and Eve and the Father: *"The man and the woman were both naked, and they felt no shame."* (Genesis 2:25)

Nakedness with no shame indicates intimacy, total and complete acceptance, nothing hidden, no fear of rejection, complete and absolute oneness. We can only imagine what that might have been like for Adam and Eve to live in total intimate oneness with one another, with all creation, and with God. Unfortunately their oneness was shattered by sin as indicated with Adam and Eve's first response to their shame: "*Then the eyes of both of them were opened and they realized they were naked; so they sewed fig leaves together and made coverings for themselves.*" (Genesis 3:7)

From that moment until today, men and women have continued to try to hide their shame. But when Jesus prayed in the shadow of His cross, He asked God to remove the shame of sin, and restore to us oneness with each other and with God. Then He stated that the result of our oneness might become our testimony to the world, "May they be brought to complete unity to let the world know that you sent me and have love*d them even as you have loved me.*"

Our intimacy with God is our testimony!

God sent Jesus to the earth to show us the divine attributes of His Father. He died on the cross to restore what sin destroyed...Oneness—Intimate Oneness with God.

Basically Jesus' prayer for us could be interpreted like this: "We've longed to reconnect with them since sin entered in. Now I am the connector. I'm connecting them to You through Me!"

That's what we are to join Christ in doing…connecting others to our Father, telling them how great His love is, how REAL His power is; and encouraging them to "Oh taste and see that the Lord, He is good!" We do this not only through our verbal testimony but through our intimacy with God. The intimacy of our relationship is our testimony.

UNWRAP THE GIFT OF HIS PRESENCE…

1. The gift of prayer is perhaps the most neglected one. Have you ever had a Christmas Day when a few gifts remain under the tree? Perhaps the recipients weren't able to make the trip home, and their gifts were to be delivered later on. Sometimes these gifts never get delivered. They are put aside and maybe forgotten. Too many times this is how God's children treat prayer—it is the amazing gift that goes unopened. Unwrap this precious gift and discover the wonder of intimacy with God.

2. I learned to pray when I prayed with other people; consider who might be a prayer partner with you.

PRAY THIS PRAYER: *Oh God, when I consider what cost You were willing to pay in order to experience intimacy with me, I am humbled. Please forgive me for taking You for granted. Teach me to pray; help me to learn to develop this intimate personal relationship with You. Amen*

CHAPTER 75

INTIMACY WITH GOD

*That all of them may be one, Father, just as you are in me
and I am in you. May they also be in us so that the world
may believe that you have sent me.*

John 17:21

Tom and I have been married more than 20 years.
We've not always been a very good picture
of Christ's relationship with His church. But
through the years we've allowed God to grow intimacy
between us. As we've grown closer to Him, we've grown
closer to one another. I dare say that much of the success
of our intentional ministry is impacted by the unintentional relationship we share. Over the years we've earned
credibility to give marriage advice—we earned the right
to be heard because our relationship speaks volumes over
what we say.

The same is true in your relationship with the Father.
You can memorize evangelistic presentations and practice
delivering them (I am 100% for this.), but your greatest
witness will be the unintentional display of the intimacy
you share with your Heavenly Father. Jesus gave His very
life for you to experience this—don't miss it.

Finally, to close this amazing prayer recorded in John

17, Jesus expressed the depth of longing and sorrow already in His heart because of His physical absence from those He loved so intimately.

Father, I want those you have given me to be with me where I am, and to see my glory, the glory you have given me because you loved me before the creation of the world. Righteous Father, though the world does not know you, I know you, and they know that you have sent me. I have made you known to them, and will continue to make you known in order that the love you have for me may be in them and that I myself may be in them. (John 17:24-26)

When I read these verses I'm reminded of these words from the hymn, *Love Is the Theme*, we sang in church when I was young:

Of the themes that men have known,
One supremely stands alone;
Thro' the ages it has shown,
'Tis His wonderful wonderful love.

Love is the theme, love is supreme;
Sweeter it grows. Glory bestows;
Bright as the sun, ever it glows!
Love is the theme, eternal theme!

Albert C. Fisher

Jesus came to earth to establish oneness with the Father. Today, He nurtures this intimacy in the same way married couples nurture their intimacy—through communication. The main purpose of prayer is to draw us into One-ness with God—to deepen our intimacy with Him.

UNWRAP THE GIFT OF HIS PRESENCE...

1. Think of a time you were especially intimate with someone—a friend, your mother or father, a child, perhaps your spouse. Where were you? What were you doing? Why did you feel so close at that moment?

2. Thank God for that person. Just say, "Thank You, Lord for _____. Thank God for that time."

PRAY THIS PRAYER: *Lord, I realize that You want time that special with me. I want that too. Thank You for Jesus' death; without His death the intimacy I desire would be impossible. Thank You for loving me so much that You would want to be intimate with me. I invite You to take me there with You. Amen*

PART 3

I'LL LEAD YOU TO THE CROSS

Just as Moses lifted up the snake in the desert,
so the Son of Man must be lifted up,
that everyone who believes in him may have eternal life.

John 3:14-15

Eventually all roads lead to the cross. Only God can take a symbol of suffering and shame and transform it into a precious representation of all that is good. Jesus told us that the cross was His destiny; it was the very reason He came.

Jesus replied, "The hour has come for the Son of Man to be glorified. I tell you the truth, unless a kernel of wheat falls to the ground and dies, it remains only a single seed. But if it dies, it produces many seeds...Now my heart is troubled, and what shall I say? 'Father save me from this hour?' No, it was for this very reason I came to this hour. Father, glorify Your name!" (John 12:23-24, 27)

In the following devotions we will visit with the people who were there at the cross the day that Jesus died. My prayer is that you will come to worship God in a fresh way as you spend this time at the cross.

CHAPTER 76

IT ALL STARTED
IN A GARDEN

*Then Jesus went with his disciples to a place called
Gethsemane, and he said to them,
"Sit here while I go over there and pray."*
Matthew 26:36

God is such a Master Designer. When He first created man He put him in a garden; a garden perfectly prepared to meet his every need and then to heap on an abundance of blessings that went far beyond the bare necessities of life.

Now the Lord God has planted a garden in the east, in Eden; and there he put the man he had formed. (Genesis 2:8)

Do you think that it was a coincidence that Jesus led His disciples to the Garden of Gethsemane the evening He was to be arrested? I don't. It all started in a garden, and God, in His omnipotent wisdom, strategically determined that it would end there as well.

In the Garden of Eden, Satan, in the form of a serpent, marched boldly to Eve and deceived her with lies. She yielded to his deception and Satan stole the crown of God's creation. In the Garden of Gethsemane Jesus took back what the Enemy stole by yielding Himself to the sovereignty of His Father. Jesus redeemed mankind by embracing the cross. It was in the Garden of Gethsemane that Jesus settled all doubt (if there was any doubt); He surrendered all fear (if the Son of Man was capable of fear); and He put His "yes" on the table before God.

My Father, if it is possible may this cup be taken from me. Yet not as I will, but as you will. (Matthew 26:39)

Jesus didn't yield to the flesh at any point. Unlike Eve, Jesus chose not to second guess His Father. He put His own life aside and accepted "the cup" God had for Him. The taste was bitter and the "juice" was not what He would have chosen for Himself. But Jesus had already told His disciples that He would never choose His own way.

For I seek not to please myself but Him who sent me. (John 5:30)

Three times Jesus prayed, and three times He committed Himself to His Father's plan. Sin's debt was paid when Jesus hung on the cross, but the victory of the cross was won when Jesus prayed in the garden.

The Garden of Eden was filled with everything we

ever needed or wanted, and we gave it up to go our own way. The Garden of Gethsemane was a tiny oasis in a world gone wrong. In that tiny oasis and completely alone, the Savior of the world, Jesus Christ, the Son of the Living God set His eyes on the cross and never looked back.

It all started in a garden.

I'LL LEAD YOU TO THE CROSS . . .

1. Many spiritual victories are won in the prayer closet. For when we enter in this quiet place we bear our souls. It's there that we determine whose cup we're willing to drink. Have you ever been to such a place? What resulted from your "garden" time?

2. What might have happened had Peter, James, and John stayed awake to pray with Jesus?

3. What might happen if you stay awake and pray?

PRAY THIS PRAYER: *Oh God, how many gardens have You invited me to visit? And how many have I passed on by? Please forgive me for the blessings I've missed. Strengthen me to join You the next time You invite me to come. Amen*

CHAPTER 77

JUDAS

And while He was still speaking, behold, Judas,
one of the twelve, came up, accompanied by a great
multitude with swords and clubs, from the chief priests and
elders of the people. Now he who was betraying Him gave
them a sign, saying, "Whomever I shall kiss, He is the one;
seize Him." And immediately he went to Jesus and said,
"Hail, Rabbi!" and kissed Him. And Jesus said to him,
"Friend, do what you have come for."
Then they came and laid hands on Jesus and seized Him.
Matthew 26:47-50 NASB

How does a man walk with Jesus for three years, listen to Him teach, witness His miracles, and experience the Presence of God in the flesh then betray Him with a kiss?

Judas must have come to follow Jesus with a preset agenda. He must have come with preconceived notions. Rather than allow Jesus to change his way of thinking, Judas must have wanted Jesus to validate his own agenda. He might have waited and watched to see if Jesus would lead a revolution to end oppression of Jews under Roman rule.

I've no way of knowing what Judas was thinking, but he was given every opportunity to change his mind. I wonder if Jesus were speaking to Judas when He warned against the treasures of this world.

Don't collect for yourselves treasures on earth, where moth and rust destroy and where thieves break in and steal. But collect for yourselves treasures in heaven, where neither moth nor rust destroys, and where thieves don't break in and steal. For where your treasure is, there your heart will be also. (Matthew 6:19-21 HCSB)

I wonder if Jesus' gaze penetrated Judas' cloud of confusion when He caught his eye as He spoke these words. Apparently Judas remained confused. Either that or he simply hadn't thought things through. According to Matthew 27:3 he was not prepared for Jesus' death sentence.

Then when Judas, who had betrayed Him, saw that He had been condemned, he felt remorse and returned the thirty pieces of silver to the chief priests and elders, saying, "I have sinned by betraying innocent blood." But they said, "What is that to us? See to that yourself!" And he threw the pieces of silver into the temple sanctuary and departed; and he went away and hanged himself. (Matthew 27:3-5 NASB)

Jesus might have not blasted the barriers erected in Judas' mind, but He'd certainly scaled the walls of his heart. Judas didn't have to betray Jesus—he chose to.

And even when he was sorry, the deed was already done. This is a sober lesson on the consequences and remorse of poor choices.

Judas' betrayal of Jesus led him to his death. Before Jesus hung on the cross, Judas hung on a tree. Jesus' death brought life. Judas' death brought absolutely nothing.

I'LL LEAD YOU TO THE CROSS . . .

1. What stood between Judas and eternal life? Pride? Arrogance? Stubborness? Tradition? A heart for this world?

2. What did these barriers do for Judas?

3. What might they do for you?

PRAY THIS PRAYER: *Oh God, I don't want to be like Judas. Give me the humility I need to have a mind that is renewed by You. Discipline me to embrace Your truth by reading Your Word daily. Amen*

CHAPTER 78

MALCHUS

*While He was still speaking, Judas, one of the Twelve,
suddenly arrived. With him was a mob, with swords and
clubs, from the chief priests, the scribes, and the elders.
His betrayer had given them a signal. "The One I kiss," he
said, "He's the One; arrest Him and take Him away under
guard." So when he came, he went right up to Him and said,
"Rabbi!"—and kissed Him. Then they took hold of Him
and arrested Him. And one of those who stood by drew his
sword, struck the high priest's slave, and cut off his ear. But
Jesus said to them, "Have you come out with swords and
clubs, as though I were a criminal, to capture Me? Every day
I was among you, teaching in the temple complex, and you
didn't arrest Me. But the Scriptures must be fulfilled."
Then they all deserted Him and ran away.*

Mark 14:43-50 HCSB

What a tense situation it must have been when the crowd arrived! Perhaps this was why Jesus asked Peter, James and John to keep watch. Can you imagine the scene? It was well past dark. Jesus and eleven of His twelve disciples were doing what they'd done many times before, just chillin' out in the garden. Andrew and Bartholomew might have been whittling pieces of olive wood. Thomas and Philip were maybe huddled up with Simon discussing the strange dinner they'd just finished sharing with Jesus. We know what Peter, James, and John were doing; they were sleeping!

Suddenly a crowd armed with swords, clubs, and spears stormed into their resting place. The disciples scrambled as the crowd surrounded them, leaving no gap where even one might escape. Then, even in the dark, Judas knew Jesus well enough to identify him with a kiss.

Then Simon Peter, who had a sword, drew it, struck the high priest's slave, and cut off his right ear. [The slave's name was Malchus.] (John 18:10 HCSB)

Malchus must have been standing next to Judas for in the split second of chaos, Peter whacked off his ear. I don't think it was Malchus' ear Peter was hoping to sever. Most likely Malchus caught sight of the sword and ducked to save his head when the sharp blade missed its mark and separated his ear from its home.

The crowd was yelling, the disciples were scrambling, and Malchus was reaching to the side of his head where his ear should have been. Jesus bent down and searched the ground for Malchus' disengaged ear. When He felt it in His hand, He scooped it up and stooped on His knees to look Malchus in the eyes. Jesus' direct gaze held the same compassion He'd shared before with the blind and deaf, the crippled and lame, the lepers and widows. And with no effort at all Jesus took Malchus' face in His hands, gently shoved Malchus' own hand away from his gaping wound, and reattached his ear so that Malchus' wife would never know it had ever been disturbed at all.

This was the last time Jesus would heal during His earthly ministry.

I wonder what Malchus thought as he escorted Jesus to the Sanhedrin that night. He might have been at the front of the line when they set out toward the garden, but I imagine he was at the back as they marched back toward home. Perhaps he walked by himself periodically reaching to feel his ear.

I don't know if Malchus was for or against the crucifixion of Jesus. But I would imagine he was fairly quiet as he watched the events unfold over the next few days.

I'LL LEAD YOU TO THE CROSS...

1. If you were Malchus, how would Jesus' kindness affect you?

2. When have you experienced the mercy and grace of God? How did it make you feel to receive His undeserved favor?

PRAY THIS PRAYER: *Lord, there is not a day that goes by that I don't receive Your mercy and grace. Like Malchus I am baffled at how You love me. Thank You for Your compassion, for Your mercy, and for Your grace. Amen*

CHAPTER 79

CAIAPHAS THE HIGH PRIEST

Those who had arrested Jesus took him to Caiaphas, the high priest, where the teachers of the law and the elders had assembled. But Peter followed him at a distance, right up to the courtyard of the high priest. He entered and sat down with the guards to see the outcome.

The chief priests and the whole Sanhedrin were looking for false evidence against Jesus so that they could put him to death. But they did not find any, though many false witnesses came forward.

Finally two came forward and declared, "This fellow said, 'I am able to destroy the temple of God and rebuild it in three days.'"

Then the high priest stood up and said to Jesus, "Are you not going to answer? What is this testimony that these men are bringing against you?" But Jesus remained silent.

The high priest said to him, "I charge you under oath by the living God: Tell us if you are the Christ, the Son of God."

"Yes, it is as you say," Jesus replied. "But I say to all of you: In the future you will see the Son of Man sitting at the right hand of the Mighty One and coming on the clouds of heaven."

Then the high priest tore his clothes and said, "He has spoken blasphemy! Why do we need any more witnesses?

Look, now you have heard the blasphemy. What do you think?"

"He is worthy of death," they answered. Then they spit in his face and struck him with their fists. Others slapped him and said, "Prophesy to us, Christ, Who hit you?"

Matthew 26:57-67

The office of high priest originated with Aaron and then passed down to his direct descendants. Privilege accompanied its position. For instance, the high priest wore special garments; kept the sacred lots (Urim and Thummim) that were used to inquire of God; and they were the only ones allowed to enter the holy of holies on the Day of Atonement. However, by this time in Israel's history, the position of high priest had deteriorated to be a position awarded by the Romans to their political favorites. According to the *Holman Bible Dictionary*, "Annas was clearly the most powerful priestly figure. Even when deposed of his priestly position by the Romans, Annas succeeded in having five of his sons and a son-in-law, Joseph Caiaphas appointed high priests."

In John's account of this dark night he tells us that the mob actually took Jesus to Annas' home first (John 18:12-13). This tells me that Annas might have been the real power behind Caiaphas' "throne." It also tells me that Caiaphas was a political favorite of the Romans, that his position was one of power and prestige over and above one of devotion; and that he was most likely a weak man who allowed his father-in-law to call the shots.

Most bullies are cowards. Caiaphas was a coward. He profaned the name of God by claiming the position of high priest. And his spiritual blindness is an indicator of the terrible stronghold that Satan weaves around the hearts and minds of people today.

Don't you see the irony of it all? Caiaphas represented the mediator—the chief mediator between God and man. His was a position rooted in sincerity and devotion to God. The original high priest, Aaron, was God's spokesperson to His people. Aaron did not consider his rank as something to be coveted for his own personal gain but rather as a sober office of mediation between a desperate people and a holy God. But Caiaphas, on the other hand, sought his position for personal gain. And even though Caiaphas most likely memorized the first five books of the Bible (something that all religious leaders did in that day), he was so blind that he completely missed God when He was standing in his presence!!

Caiaphas blasphemed God at the very moment he accused Jesus of blasphemy. I would imagine it was better for Judas than it was for Caiaphas when he met his Maker.

I'LL LEAD YOU TO THE CROSS . . .

1. Do you know people like Caiaphas today? People that are students of God's Word but who've lost their love and devotion to God?

2. What might keep you from being blinded by religion, prestige, and power?

PRAY THIS PRAYER: *Father, please forgive me for claiming to know more than I know, and for being full of pride in Your holy presence. Please show me where I'm guilty of being led by ambition and an unhealthy desire for power. Remind me today that those who are great in Your eyes are those who are small in the eyes of the world. Let me be tiny, Lord. Amen*

CHAPTER 80

PETER'S PROMISE

Then Jesus said to them, "Tonight all of you will run away
and stumble because of Me, for it is written: I will strike
the shepherd, and the sheep of the flock will be scattered.
But after I have been resurrected, I will go ahead of you
to Galilee." Peter told Him, "Even if everyone runs away
because of You, I will never run away!" "I assure you,"
Jesus said to him, "tonight—before the rooster crows, you
will deny Me three times!" "Even if I have to die with You,"
Peter told Him, "I will never deny You!"
And all the disciples said the same thing.

Matthew 26:31-35 HCSB

Did you notice the last sentence in that passage of Scripture? Peter was the one who declared his undying devotion to Christ, but that last sentence says that "all the disciples said the same thing." Why is it that we shake our heads at Peter?

Peter was a leader. Jesus had already endorsed Peter's leadership in the presence of the twelve; and with that endorsement Jesus gave Peter authority and power.

When Jesus came to the region of Caesarea Philippi, He asked His disciples, "Who do people say that the Son of Man is?"

And they said, "Some say John the Baptist; others, Elijah; still others, Jeremiah or one of the prophets." "But you," He asked them, "who do you say that I am?" Simon Peter answered, "You are the Messiah, the Son of the living God!" And Jesus responded, "Simon son of Jonah, you are blessed because flesh and blood did not reveal this to you, but My Father in heaven. And I also say to you that you are Peter, and on this rock I will build My church, and the forces of Hades will not over-power it. I will give you the keys of the kingdom of heaven, and whatever you bind on earth is already bound in heaven, and whatever you loose on earth is already loosed in heaven." (Matthew 16:13-19 HCSB)

So when the rest of the disciples deserted Jesus, much less is said of their failure than what is said of Peter's. That's how it is with leadership. For those of you who are leaders, God expects you to lead. For those of you who are followers, God expects you to follow.

Was Peter speaking out of order that night at dinner? I don't think so. He was simply being Peter. Peter was a man's man. He was a warrior at heart and full of passion! When he chose to follow Jesus, he didn't simply engage his head—he jumped completely into discipleship with his whole heart. Peter grew to love Jesus passionately, and he was dedicated to doing whatever it took to see that Jesus was safe.

This zeal to "protect" Jesus earned him a severe rebuke:

From that time Jesus began to show His disciples that He must go to Jerusalem, and suffer many things from the elders and chief priests and scribes, and be killed, and be raised up on the third day. Peter took Him aside and began to rebuke Him, saying, "God forbid it, Lord! This shall never happen to You." But He turned and said to Peter, "Get behind Me, Satan! You are a stumbling block to Me; for you are not setting your mind on God's interests, but man's." (Matthew 16:21-23 NASB)

So at the dinner table that night, the news that Jesus was going to die was not "new." Peter and the others had heard that word before. Not only had Jesus spelled it out, but they too were already living in an atmosphere of suspicion, uncertainty, and fear.

During the Feast of Dedication, the Jews almost stoned him for blasphemy (see John 10:22-40). It was because of that scary ordeal that Thomas said what he said when Jesus told His disciples He was going to see Lazarus.

Then Thomas (called Didymus) said to the rest of the disciples, "Let us go, that we may die with him." (John 11:16)

Peter's promise was as sincere as Thomas' had been that day. If Peter couldn't save Jesus from death, he sincerely meant to die with Him. But God had other plans.

I'LL LEAD YOU TO THE CROSS . . .

1. Take a few minutes to imagine how dangerous it had become to be a disciple of Christ. Think of the devotion of Jesus' followers.

2. Have you ever promised something you were unable to deliver? How did that make you feel?

PRAY THIS PRAYER: *Lord, thank You for making me a leader/follower. Help me to fulfill my role well. Teach me to think before I speak and to share the passion for You that Peter shared. I want to be used by You just as Peter was used. Amen*

CHAPTER 81

PETER'S ATTEMPT TO MAKE GOOD ON HIS PROMISE

*Then Simon Peter, who had a sword, drew it and struck
the high priest's servant, cutting off his right ear.
(The servant's name was Malchus.) Jesus commanded
Peter, "Put your sword away! Shall I not drink
the cup the Father has given me?"*

John 18:10-11

*At that time Jesus said to the crowd, "Am I leading a
rebellion that you have come out with swords and clubs to
capture me? Every day I sat in the temple courts teaching,
and you did not arrest me. But this has all taken place that
the writings of the prophets might be fulfilled." Then all the
disciples deserted him and fled.*

*But Peter followed him at a distance, right up to the
courtyard of the high priest. He entered and sat down with the
guards to see the outcome. (Matthew 26:55-56, 58)*

We tend to think a lot about how Peter denied Jesus three times just before the rooster
crowed (like Jesus said he would), but we
sometimes miss all that Peter did before that. When the

mob came to the garden, Peter took out his sword and chopped Malchus' ear off! (I've already suggested that Peter most likely wasn't aiming for that right ear.) Then, when all the other disciples went one direction, only Peter and John went another. They were the only two who actually followed Him all the way into the courtyard of the high priest.

Have you ever been surprised by the fervor of your devotion to God? I have. The morning I woke up before it was light to the sound of Muslim prayers in Bangalore, India, I was surprised at where my devotion took me. The day I shared a message through a translator in a concrete pavilion in Nicaragua I was surprised at where my love for Jesus took me.

Peter loved Jesus. He was willing to go with Him to the grave. Right there in the Garden of Gethsemane where he was ridiculously outnumbered and overpowered, Peter took his sword out of his belt and took a swing at the servant of the high priest! But notice what happened when he did that,

Jesus commanded Peter, "Put your sword away! Shall I not drink the cup the Father has given me?" (John 18:11)

I can almost feel something die in Peter when Jesus commanded him to stop. Think about that word, "commanded." I don't think Jesus used His kindest tone with Peter at that moment. To be "commanded" means to be shouted at, to be rebuked, to be spoken to harshly. How frustrating was that? I don't have a hard time wondering at why Peter followed him at a distance and hid in the courtyard like a spy. I don't think he knew what else to do.

I'LL LEAD YOU TO THE CROSS . . .

1. Have you ever had to shrink back from what you thought God wanted you to do and simply wait in the shadows to regroup?

2. How might Peter have made good on his promise to Jesus? Why is it better that he didn't?

PRAY THIS PRAYER: *Father, teach me to trust You. Teach me to look beyond the circumstances and to see Your bigger picture—to live for the resurrection moment when all that You've promised comes true. Amen*

CHAPTER 82

PETER'S DENIAL

*Now Peter was sitting outside in the courtyard, and a
servant-girl came to him and said, "You too were with Jesus
the Galilean." But he denied it before them all, saying,
"I do not know what you are talking about." When he had
gone out to the gateway, another servant-girl saw him and
said to those who were there, "This man was with Jesus of
Nazareth." And again he denied it with an oath, "I do not
know the man." A little later the bystanders came up and
said to Peter, "Surely you too are one of them; for even the
way you talk gives you away." Then he began to curse and
swear, "I do not know the man!" And immediately
a rooster crowed. And Peter remembered the word which
Jesus had said, "Before a rooster crows, you will deny Me
three times." And he went out and wept bitterly.*

Matthew 26:69-75 NASB

L eave it to the servant girls to blow Peter's cover.
Isn't it just like girls to do that? Peter was sitting in
the courtyard when they began to recognize him as
having been with Jesus. His secret was in serious danger
of being discovered when he opened his mouth to speak,
for one of the bystanders recognized his voice and said,
"even the way you talk gives you away!"

Think about that for a minute. If you were sitting in enemy territory, would bystanders and servant girls smell Jesus on you? Would your time with Jesus give you away? What about your words or the way you deliver them? Would an innocent bystander declare, "even the way you talk gives you away!" Oh, that it would be so!

But why, when Peter had already declared his allegiance to Jesus and had even before put himself in harm's way…why now, would he deny Christ? Perhaps Peter, like so many of us, found it much easier to do what his heart told him was right when he was surrounded by friends and when he was in a safe place.

When Peter made his promise, he was sitting in a room encircled by 11 men with whom he'd shared life for the past three years. Jesus washed his feet (an act that proved extremely humbling to Peter), and was sharing an intimate dinner with him. In this setting Peter felt deep love, respect, honor, and oneness (or intimacy) with Christ. It was in this place that Peter made his promise.

Haven't you been there too? Perhaps it was a worship service or a prayer time or even at camp or a retreat. It's a holy place where you are resting in the love, wonder, and awe of God. You pledge your allegiance. Your "yes" is on the table! There's nothing you won't do for Christ.

When Peter drew his sword he was still surrounded by 10 of the 11 men with whom he'd shared his life. He'd just let Jesus down by sleeping when Jesus asked him to "keep watch and pray." So when the mob approached Jesus, Peter quickly drew his sword almost without thinking because it was his duty and his call! I've been there too. At church or on a mission trip eager to "do" what God called me to "do" only to discover that I should have been "keeping watch and praying" so I would know when to draw my sword and when to walk away.

And then Peter was in the courtyard. He was no doubt confused, mad at himself, and angry at the world. What was happening to Jesus was out of his control, and even Jesus wouldn't do anything about it. So when the servant girls began to wag their tongues, he denied knowing the man he promised to protect.

Peter denied his Lord. We might have done the same—no friends for support; terribly confused...Peter was all alone in a dreadful place. And when the rooster crowed, Peter remembered what Jesus had said and, "he went outside and wept bitterly."

I'LL LEAD YOU TO THE CROSS . . .

1. Have you ever been in a place where you hoped no one would realize you were a Christian? Why were you there? How did it feel?

2. Has God ever confused you? What did you do when that happened?

PRAY THIS PRAYER: *Precious Savior, remind me that when I am confused I need to stay close to others who know and love You. Help me to make good on my promises to You, and to never suffer the bitterness of letting You down. But if I do, bring me back like You brought Peter back. Amen*

CHAPTER 83

PETER AT THE CROSS

So Peter and the other disciple started for the tomb.
Both were running but the other disciple outran Peter and
reached the tomb first. He bent over and looked in at the
strips of linen lying but did not go in. Then Simon Peter,
who was behind him, arrived and went into the tomb.
He saw the strips of linen lying there, as well as the burial
cloth that had been around Jesus' head.
The cloth was folded up by itself, separate from the linen.
John 20:3-7

There is no Scripture that tells us that Peter was at the cross when Jesus died...none. I think he was there—just on the outskirts watching helplessly with swollen eyes and a broken heart. I think that if the servant girls had seen him they wouldn't have recognized him at all.

But we just don't know for sure. What we do know is that Peter was the first one to rush right into Jesus' empty tomb. He and John gave us a great description of what he found there. But the moment Peter came to the cross was that morning by the sea.

He and the other fishermen/disciples didn't know what else to do after Jesus' death so they just went back to what they'd done before. They went fishing. I love this fishing story. They caught nothing all night. The fish weren't biting when Jesus called to them from the beach and urged them to put their nets on the other side of the boat. When they followed His suggestion, they caught the biggest load of fish they'd ever caught—but that's not what thrilled them. Immediately they recognized Jesus. Peter was so eager to see His Lord that he jumped out of the boat and swam to shore where Jesus was already cooking breakfast. (This is the second time Peter jumped out of a boat.)

I love how God knows to tap into our physical senses. The night that Peter was in Caiaphas' courtyard, Scripture records that the servants and officials were warming themselves by a fire. Imagine the sound of that fire as the flames leaped over the coals. Imagine the smell of the charcoal burning in the cold night. As soon as Peter waded to shore the smell of Jesus' cooking fire must have triggered the bitterness that still remained from the memory of the fire he'd smelled just days before.

After breakfast Jesus and Peter talked. It was more than reconciliation; it was a *calling*. Peter had to answer Jesus three times when He asked him if he loved Him because he'd denied Him three times before. The declaration of Peter's love wasn't to reassure Jesus, even Peter knew this, *"you know that I love you…Yes, Lord, you know that I love you…Lord, you know all things; you know that I love you."*

Peter declared his love for Jesus three times to reassure himself. Jesus wanted to get the bitterness of Peter's failure behind him for Jesus had work for Peter to do.

"Feed my lambs…Take care of my sheep…Feed my sheep."

When we fail God, He brings us back to Himself with His tender compassion. But when we are restored, He expects us to look back no more. Instead Jesus calls each one of us to get on with the business of feeding His sheep.

I'LL LEAD YOU TO THE CROSS . . .

1. Have you disappointed God? Why not spend some time with Him and let Him help you make that right.

2. What specific work did God give you to do? How are you doing in your task?

PRAY THIS PRAYER: *Lord, You know all things; You know that I love You. I'm willing to do whatever Your love demands. Amen*

CHAPTER 84

PONTIUS PILATE

*After tying Him up, they led Him away
and handed Him over to Pilate, the governor.*
Matthew 27:2 HCSB

*Then they took Jesus from Caiaphas to the governor's
headquarters. It was early morning. They did not enter the
headquarters themselves; otherwise they would be defiled and
unable to eat the Passover. Then Pilate came out to them and
said, "What charge do you bring against this man?" They
answered him, "If this man weren't a criminal, we wouldn't
have handed Him over to you." So Pilate told them, "Take
Him yourselves and judge Him according to your law." "It's
not legal for us to put anyone to death," the Jews declared.
They said this so that Jesus' words might be fulfilled signifying
what sort of death He was going to die. (John 18:28-32
HCSB)*

Pontius Pilate was the Roman governor of Judea
(called a procurator in documents other than the
New Testament). He was anti-Semitic (along with
his contemporaries in Rome and Egypt) and issued many
edicts intended to inflict persecution on the Jews. That
fact alone makes it unusual that he allowed himself to be

pressured by Jewish religious authorities into having Jesus crucified. He must have been insecure in his position both with the Jewish leaders and with Rome.

Since the Jewish leaders brought Jesus to him early in the morning (and refused to enter his palace because of their Passover laws), Pilate was most likely annoyed by them before he ever left his poached eggs and pomegranate juice to meet them.

You can almost hear the disdain the Jewish leaders had for this "enemy" governor in the way they answered his inquiry; their response dripped with sarcasm.

"What charges are you bringing against this man?"

"If he were not a criminal, we would not have handed him over to you."

Pilate tried to get them to go away by giving them the right to judge Jesus themselves. That's when the chief priests and all their cohorts said an unusual thing: "But we have no right to execute anyone."

If this was the case, why did they bring the woman caught in adultery to the temple courts, set her before Jesus, and pick up stones to throw at her? (John 8:1-11) Why did they try to stone Jesus during the Feast of Dedication? (John 10:31-39) The Jews had killed their own before and apparently hadn't gotten in trouble for doing so. But they couldn't crucify anyone, and they had in their minds to crucify Jesus. Of course John clarifies the truth that while the Jewish leaders thought they were orchestrating their own plans for Jesus, a Power much greater than theirs was setting all the details in motion.

This happened so that the words Jesus had spoken indicating the kind of death he was going to die would be fulfilled. (John 18:32)

I'LL LEAD YOU TO THE CROSS . . .

1. Do you ever get discouraged because the circumstances around you seem out of control? I have a friend that quotes my husband, saying "God has already been to your tomorrows." And I'll add to that another one of his quotes, "Whatever is over your head is still under His feet."

2. How has God surprised you in the details of your life?

PRAY THIS PRAYER: *Father, open my eyes today to see my life's circumstances from Your perspective. Help me to rest in the deep understanding that You are in control. Amen*

CHAPTER 85

PILATE'S PERSONAL PURSUIT

Then Pilate went back into the headquarters,
summoned Jesus, and said to Him,
"Are You the King of the Jews?"
John 18:33 HCSB

I kind of feel sorry for Pilate. I can't help but wonder if he'd been in another time and another place if he would have had the opportunity to really follow Jesus. But nonetheless, this was Pilate's one and only encounter with Jesus, and he, like all the rest of us, had the free will to make his own choice.

After the Jewish leaders dumped Jesus on his doorstep, Pilate took Him inside and began to question Him. I can almost imagine Pilate picking the food from between his teeth with a toothpick as he leaned back in his judgment seat and proceeded with his questioning, "So…are You the King of the Jews?"

Jesus didn't answer directly—He rarely did. Jesus was forever trying to get men to dig deeper and figure out the answer to that question on their own. So instead of giving Pilate a simple "yes" or "no," He countered with a question of His own, "Is that your own idea, or did others talk to you about me?"

Although Pilate ruled over thousands, Jesus wasn't interested in what he thought as a ruler, he wanted to know what he thought as an ordinary man. In fact, when we get to heaven that's going to be the question we all have to answer, "What did *you* do with Jesus?"

But Pilate was put off, his hatred for Jews rose in him, and he merely replied with, "Am I a Jew? It was your people and your chief priests who handed you over to me. What is it you have done?"

And then Jesus gave Pilate one of the most straightforward and simple truths that He ever spoke. There are no riddles, no hidden agendas, just pure simple truth, "My kingdom is not of this world. If it were, my servants would fight to prevent my arrest by the Jews. But now my kingdom is from another place."

It's funny to me what Pilate said next because I am thinking there's no mockery in his tone. I think it's an "ah ha" moment! Not "ah ha" I've found fault in you and can put you to death for high treason, but "ah ha! I *knew* there was something majestic and royal about you!"

Jesus rewarded Pilate's declaration of faith with another straightforward honest truth, "You are right in saying I am a king. In fact, for this reason I was born, and for this I came into the world to testify to the truth. Everyone on the side of truth listens to me."

And that's where Pilate started back pedaling. With hints of depression he stated, "What is truth?"

I'LL LEAD YOU TO THE CROSS . . .

1. Can you imagine having that kind of deep and personal audience with Jesus? What would you have done if you'd been Pilate?

2. Why do you think Pilate did what he did?

PRAY THIS PRAYER: *Lord, thank You that Pilate was wrong. We can know TRUTH, and Jesus is His Name. Thank You for revealing Your Truth to me. Thank You for leading me in all Truth and thank You for embracing the cross so that the Truth could set me free. Amen*

CHAPTER 86

PILATE'S PROBLEM

At the festival the governor's custom was to release to the crowd a prisoner they wanted. At that time they had a notorious prisoner called Barabbas. So when they had gathered together, Pilate said to them, "Who is it you want me to release for you—Barabbas, or Jesus who is called Messiah?" For he knew they had handed Him over because of envy. While he was sitting on the judge's bench, his wife sent word to him, "Have nothing to do with that righteous man, for today I've suffered terribly in a dream because of Him!"

The chief priests and the elders, however, persuaded the crowds to ask for Barabbas and to execute Jesus. The governor asked them, "Which of the two do you want me to release for you?" "Barabbas!" they answered. Pilate asked them, "What should I do then with Jesus, who is called Messiah?" They all answered, "Crucify Him!" Then he said, "Why? What has He done wrong?" But they kept shouting, "Crucify Him!" all the more. When Pilate saw that he was getting nowhere, but that a riot was starting instead, he took some water, washed his hands in front of the crowd, and said, "I am innocent of this man's blood. See to it yourselves!" All the people answered, "His blood be on us and on our children!" Then he released Barabbas to them. But after having Jesus flogged, he handed Him over to be crucified.

Matthew 27:15-26 HCSB

Pilate was so close to making a truly heroic decision when he sat on that judge's bench. Even his wife encouraged him, for she'd been warned in a dream that Jesus' death would haunt him the rest of his life. But when push came to shove, Pilate couldn't do it. He couldn't resist the crowd, and he caved in to the pressure of the people.

Oh, Pilate tried to absolve himself of any wrong doing by washing his hands in front of the angry mob. But washing his hands did absolutely nothing to remove his guilt. There's only one way to remove the guilty stain of sin, and that is through the blood of Jesus Christ.

I wonder if Pilate ever met Jesus at the cross. He was the Roman ruler who sent Him there, but I wonder if ever, maybe even later on in his life, he ever went there himself. I doubt it. History records that Pilate was removed from his office because of his harsh treatment of the Samaritans. (Holman Bible Dictionary)

It is hard for us to wrap our minds around the significance of Pilate's role in Jesus' crucifixion. It's hard to imagine a government that crucifies people at all! We have a court system, an appeal process and juries of peers that execute judgment worthy of death. But in Jesus' day one man got to choose life or death.

Of course some would say that Pilate had to send Jesus to the cross—that he had no choice, that he was simply a pawn in the hand of God. But I don't believe that.

Pilate had the same opportunity everyone has. And when I read John's account of his interaction with Jesus I am sad. I'm sad that Pilate was so close—and yet so far away.

I'LL LEAD YOU TO THE CROSS . . .

1. Who do you know that sits in a seat of judgment? I just returned from a trip to Washington, DC, where I asked one of my congressmen how we might pray for him. He said that the greatest danger in Washington was PMS. P—Power, M—Money, S—Sex.

2. My congressman said that men in Washington, even good men can often be rendered ineffective for the kingdom with those three things. We need to pray for our leaders; those in Washington, DC, those who serve in our states, the ones who lead our communities, and most certainly the leaders in our churches. Make a list of men and women who need your prayers and commit to praying for them daily.

PRAY THIS PRAYER: *Father, protect me from being swayed by the crowd the way Pilate was swayed. Let me always do what is right even when I'm afraid to do it. I commit today to pray for those in leadership positions. Amen*

CHAPTER 87

THE ROMAN OFFICERS

Then the governor's soldiers took Jesus into headquarters
and gathered the whole company around Him.
They stripped Him and dressed Him in a scarlet robe.
They twisted together a crown of thorns, put it on His head,
and placed a reed in His right hand. And they knelt down
before Him and mocked Him: "Hail, King of the Jews!"
Then they spit at Him, took the reed, and kept hitting
Him on the head. When they had mocked Him,
they stripped Him of the robe, put His clothes on Him,
and led Him away to crucify Him.
Matthew 27:27-31 HCSB

This was not the first group of men to mock and beat Jesus. Don't forget that when He was at Caiaphas' house the guards that were with Him there blindfolded Him then beat Him and mocked Him saying "Prophesy! Who hit you?" And according to Luke, "they said many other insulting things to him" (Luke 22:63-65).

What makes men animals? I've often wondered that. Is it the tension of being made to live under the absolute command of others? Does wicked animal cruelty spew forth when men with physical strength are so subdued that they feel like they have to release their pent up aggression on weaker (or in this case innocent) men?

In the movie *The Passion of the Christ* I had to close my eyes during this part. In fact, I closed my eyes during most of that movie. I couldn't stand to see men mock, beat, spit on, and abuse the precious lamb of God. It was too hard to witness. How could mankind be so vile?

On 9/11 my son TJ watched the news. He was only six years old, and I probably should've shielded him from the visual of the terrorist planes flying into the World Trade Center towers. He sat in front of the television that afternoon and just watched in horror as they crashed over and over and over again. We were all in shock! But a few days later he brought home his daily journal page from school. The pages for his daily journal had a large space at the top for a picture and a few dotted lines at the bottom for a brief caption. This is how his teacher taught her class to journal their thoughts and feelings.

TJ's page had a picture of a plane flying into a tower and flames bursting out from the impact. The caption below the picture printed on those wide lines that provide dashes for penmanship said this, "Why can't we get along with each others?"

We can't because of *sin*. That ugly, painful, sick, and cruel word that sums up all selfishness and conceit, all anger and resentment, all bitterness and malice, all pride and defeat. The Roman officers went beyond their "call of duty" (which would have been more than enough in carrying out the penalty of the cross) and made sport of Jesus because they epitomized the base carnality of sin.

I can't help but wonder how those soldiers felt that night when they laid their heads down in their barracks. Did even one relive the haunting eyes of Jesus as He gazed from swollen lids into his soul with pure love and deep sorrow? Did even one soldier wonder how a man could be so mild and yet so mighty as He was beaten to a pulp? Or were they all so cold, so callous, and so tainted by sin that they closed their eyes and slept soundly?

I'll Lead You to the Cross . . .

1. Do you remember 9/11? How did you respond?

2. What do you think makes men act that way? Do you know of people who are abused today? How can you pray for them?

Pray this prayer: *Oh God forgive us for being so sin-stained and ugly. Before I go pointing my fingers at these soldiers, let me see the sin that makes me callous to the desperate needs of others. Keep my heart tender and my mind sensitive to the pain in the world and show me how I can do my part. Amen*

CHAPTER 88

HEROD

*When Pilate heard it, he asked whether the man
was a Galilean. And when he learned that He
belonged to Herod's jurisdiction, he sent Him to Herod,
who himself also was in Jerusalem at that time.
Now Herod was very glad when he saw Jesus; for he
had wanted to see Him for a long time, because he had
been hearing about Him and was hoping to see some sign
performed by Him. And he questioned Him at some length;
but He answered him nothing. And the chief priests and
the scribes were standing there, accusing Him vehemently.
And Herod with his soldiers, after treating Him with
contempt and mocking Him, dressed Him in
a gorgeous robe and sent Him back to Pilate.
Now Herod and Pilate became
friends with one another that very day;
for before they had been enemies with each other.*
Luke 23:6-12 NASB

Luke included this visit with Herod in his account
of Jesus' trial. Nothing much came of it; that's most
likely why the other gospel writers left it out. But
because Pilate was desperate to rid himself of the problem of Jesus, upon hearing of Jesus' Galilean heritage, he

quickly sent Jesus to Herod (who was ruler over Galilee). It was a classic example of passing the buck.

According to Luke 23:8, Herod was excited to meet Jesus, "...for a long time he had been wanting to see him." But Herod didn't have deep spiritual interest in Jesus at all. He was merely eager for some entertainment: "From what he had heard about him, he hoped to see him perform some miracle." Jesus knew Herod's heart. That's why He didn't answer any of Herod's questions. Where Jesus spoke openly and honestly with Pilate, Jesus didn't say a single word to Herod.

History records that Herod was one of the cruelest rulers of the time. He killed all of his heirs, including his beloved wife, for fear that one of them might cheat him of the throne. He even gave the orders to execute Antipater while he himself was on his deathbed five days prior to his own death (information from *Holman Bible Dictionary*). King Herod was the one who also had John the Baptist beheaded (Mark 6:14-29). Herod was a wicked, harsh ruler who obviously had already gone too far in sin to be reached by any word of truth. Note that Herod's soldiers did "ridicule and mock" Jesus. Then they dressed Him in an elegant robe and sent Him back to Pilate. And that was the day that Herod and Pilate became friends; a curious friendship that must have been.

Many lost people are perched precariously between Pilate and Herod. Some of them are still interested in discovering truth—yet unwilling to receive it (Pilate), while others have already been given over to the "depravity of their minds" (Herod).

I'LL LEAD YOU TO THE CROSS . . .

1. Read Romans 1:21-32. Notice that the first step toward total depravity is a neglect of worship. Spend some time worshiping God right now.

2. Do you have family members or friends who are dangerously close to becoming like Herod? If so pray for them today!

PRAY THIS PRAYER: *Oh God, there are so many in our world who have already been given over to their own depraved minds. Please let this not be so in my home. I ask that You pour on us a fresh anointing of Your Spirit and a fresh love for Your Son.*
Amen

CHAPTER 89

SIMON FROM CYRENE

*Then, willing to gratify the crowd, Pilate released Barabbas
to them. And after having Jesus flogged, he handed Him
over to be crucified. Then the soldiers led Him away into
the courtyard (that is, headquarters) and called the whole
company together. They dressed Him in a purple robe,
twisted together a crown of thorns, and put it on Him.
And they began to salute Him, "Hail, King of the Jews!"
They kept hitting Him on the head with a reed and spitting
on Him. Getting down on their knees, they were paying Him
homage. When they had mocked Him, they stripped Him of
the purple robe, put His clothes on Him, and led Him out to
crucify Him. They forced a man coming in from the country,
who was passing by, to carry Jesus' cross. He was Simon,
a Cyrenian, the father of Alexander and Rufus.*

Mark 15:15-21 HCSB

I wonder what Simon might have thought when the
Roman soldiers grabbed him by the arm and shoved
him toward Jesus. I've no doubt that as Jesus was being
led to Golgotha, the cross beam He was required to carry
was too heavy for Him to bear. After all, He'd gone an entire night with no sleep, and been tried before Caiaphas,
the chief priests, Pilate, and Herod. He'd been mocked,

spit on, hit with fists, beat with reeds, dressed in robes, and crowned with thorns by the guards of the Sanhedrin, the soldiers of Herod, and the officers of Rome. On top of that, Jesus had been flogged. The flogging alone was enough to kill him.

So on His way out of Jerusalem His broken body fell beneath the weight of the cross. Simon was most likely traveling into Jerusalem to purchase goods for his family. The fact that he was the father of Alexander and Rufus makes me wonder if Alexander and Rufus became believers and followers of Christ. Perhaps they were young boys accompanying their father on his errand. Maybe they saw the fierce Roman soldiers take hold of their father and command him to bear the weight of Jesus' cross.

Simon couldn't have possibly known who Jesus was or what He'd been accused of doing. He might have thought Him a terrible criminal for He'd obviously suffered the full brunt of Rome's cruel power. Most likely Simon was young and strong—he looked like a man who could bear Christ's cross.

What must that have felt like to Simon? Did he know that Jesus bore so much more than a cross? When the soldiers lifted the heavy cross beam from Jesus' shredded shoulders did Simon understand that it wasn't the weight of the wood that pressed Jesus down? Would Simon have had any way of knowing the sin that cross represented to Christ?

Imagine Simon following Jesus on that path. Maybe he whispered encouragement as the reality of crucifixion dug into his own flesh. "You can do this, man. Whatever you've done—be sure that it's over soon; you can make it, I know you can." Alexander and Rufus might have been tempted to heckle Jesus with the others, but I think Simon made them stop.

"Hey, what'd you do, kill somebody?"

"I bet you beat a Roman soldier; what were you thinking?"

"Alexander…[deep breath]…Rufus! Stop that. You know nothing about this man and have no right to pass judgment. Be quiet and stay close," Simon might have said.

And then when they got to Golgotha I like to think that Simon saw just enough to begin a pursuit that ended with his conversion. I can't imagine what it might have been like to bear the weight of Jesus' cross.

I'LL LEAD YOU TO THE CROSS . . .

1. If you'll take time to really ponder the people who spent Good Friday with Jesus, you just might capture a bit of their story. This is all pretend but worth the effort.

2. What kind deed might you do for your Savior today?

PRAY THIS PRAYER: *Lord, thank You for men like Simon who completed a simple task. Let me be about the simple task of doing whatever it is that You have for me to do today. Amen*

CHAPTER 90

CHIEF PRIEST AND SCRIBES

Those passing by were hurling abuse at Him, wagging their
heads, and saying, "Ha! You who are going to destroy the
temple and rebuild it in three days, save Yourself, and come
down from the cross!" In the same way the chief priests also,
along with the scribes, were mocking Him among themselves
and saying, "He saved others; He cannot save Himself.
Let this Christ, the King of Israel, now come down from
the cross, so that we may see and believe." Those who were
crucified with Him were also insulting Him.

Mark 15:29-32 NASB

And those passing by were hurling abuse at Him, wagging
their heads and saying, "You who are going to destroy the
temple and rebuild it in three days, save Yourself! If You
are the Son of God, come down from the cross." In the
same way the chief priests also, along with the scribes and
elders, were mocking Him and saying, "He saved others;
He cannot save Himself. He is the King of Israel; let Him
now come down from the cross, and we will believe in Him.
He trusts in God; let God rescue him now, if he delights in
him; for He said, 'I am the Son of God.'" The robbers who
had been crucified with Him were also insulting Him with the
same words. (Matthew 27:39-44 NASB)

I can almost understand the crowd hurling abuse at Jesus...almost. They were most likely small-minded people who were not thinking and certainly unaware of who Jesus was. They were just a few steps away from being as grossly sin-stained as the soldiers who mocked, beat, and spit on Jesus. But when I see the chief priests and scribes joining in, I'm somewhat surprised.

Weren't these men the religious leaders of the day? Weren't they the students of the books of the Law? Didn't they commit the Pentateuch (first five books of the Old Testament) to memory? And weren't they the ones who interpreted Scripture for others to follow?

These were the men who stood up to teach in the synagogues and who discussed and executed judgment on issues regarding the mosaic law. They called themselves representatives of Jehovah! And here they are at the cross hurling insults and mocking Him! How could they be so blind?

In order to answer that question, we need to look at Matthew 23:25-28 (NASB).

"Woe to you, scribes and Pharisees, hypocrites! For you clean the outside of the cup and of the dish, but inside they are full of robbery and self-indulgence. You blind Pharisee, first clean the inside of the cup and of the dish, so that the outside of it may become clean also. Woe to you, scribes and Pharisees, hypocrites! For you are like whitewashed tombs which on the

outside appear beautiful, but inside they are full of dead men's bones and all uncleanness. So you, too, outwardly appear righteous to men, but inwardly you are full of hypocrisy and lawlessness."

According to Jesus, the Pharisees, chief priests, scribes, and Sadducees were blind because they were corrupt from the inside. I would have thought that out of simple regard for morality the chief priests and scribes would stand toward the back of the crowd and be quiet about their success. But no! They didn't have any shred of human decency in them! They were so eat up with self-righteousness, indulgence, hypocrisy, and greed that they pressed their arrogant selves right up to the foot of the cross and wagged their evil tongues.

I'LL LEAD YOU TO THE CROSS . . .

1. Scripture has much to teach us regarding the enemies of Christ. We would do well to ask, "How am I like the Pharisees?" so that we don't grow deaf and dumb.

2. Is there any hypocrisy in you? If so, confess it to the Lord; repent and determine to change today.

PRAY THIS PRAYER: *Oh Lord, my precious Savior and Redeemer, please guard my heart. I don't want to be a hypocrite. Squeeze self-righteousness, indulgence, and greed out of me. Make me a servant pleasing to You. Amen*

CHAPTER 91

THE ROBBERS

Then one of the criminals hanging there began to yell insults at Him: "Aren't You the Messiah? Save Yourself and us!" But the other answered, rebuking him: "Don't you even fear God, since you are undergoing the same punishment? We are punished justly, because we're getting back what we deserve for the things we did, but this man has done nothing wrong."

Then he said, "Jesus, remember me when You come into Your kingdom!" And He said to him, "I assure you: Today you will be with Me in paradise."

Luke 23:39-43 HCSB

We sometimes forget the other two men who hung on either side of Jesus that day. We don't really care about their demise; after all they deserved to die. Nevertheless, they were suffering the same horrendous death as Jesus.

Luke records an interesting conversation that took place among the three of them. One of the criminals joined in with the mob, the chief priests, and soldiers and mocked Jesus along with the rest. You've met people like him. Maybe his mother fed him artichokes for breakfast, or perhaps his Dad made him sleep on tacks. Whatever it was, he was mean before he hit puberty. He most likely stole a bag of gold or cheated a merchant out of his merchandise. He felt no remorse, and even when death stared him in the face he was too callous to care. He had no regard for God nor man.

"Aren't you the Messiah? Save yourself, and while you're at it, get us off these crosses too!" he mocked Jesus.

But the other thief was different. Maybe his walk to Golgotha gave him some time to think. Perhaps his conscience was not quite dead, and something in the way Jesus quietly endured the pain sparked an ember of faith in his guilt-ridden heart. He hung there, watching, taking note that Jesus was evidently someone famous. He might have seen the women crying and noticed the haggard looks on the faces of Galilean fishermen who lingered about the edges of the crowd just behind the chief priests and scribes. He'd never had any respect for those Jewish religious leaders anyway, and so their mocking of Jesus didn't surprise him.

And as this thief hung in midair, pressing against the spike in his ankles to lift his body for the next excruciating breath, he recognized something strangely and wonderfully different about Jesus. So when the other thug launched his own abuse from across the way, this thief solemnly responded, "Don't you even fear God, since you are undergoing the same punishment? We are punished justly, because we're getting back what we deserve for the things we did, but this man has done nothing wrong."

Then he might have paused long enough to strain again against the iron that ripped through the ligaments and tendons in his ankles just so he could take another breath. And as he breathed, I think he looked at Jesus and quietly asked, "Remember me when you enter into your kingdom."

What a beautiful statement of faith! Right there, being crucified like a common criminal, this one man saw what others missed. He saw that Jesus was the King of kings and Lord of lords. I can only barely begin to imagine how his heart must have rested when he heard Jesus' sweet response, "I assure you: Today you will be with Me in paradise."

If there was any doubt that we don't add anything to our salvation, let this story put that to rest. The only thing I add to my salvation is the sin that put Jesus on the cross. Heaven is a free gift—we simply believe and receive.

I'LL LEAD YOU TO THE CROSS . . .

1. Why do people think that we have to "do something" to be saved?

2. What do you think happened the minute this thief took his final breath? What must that have been like to be escorted into heaven with the Son of God?

PRAY THIS PRAYER: *Lord, thank You that the thief believed. He gives me hope for [name someone who seems hopeless]. I ask that You open their eyes so that they too might be with You in paradise. Amen*

CHAPTER 92

THE CENTURION

It was now about noon, and darkness came over the whole
land until three, because the sun's light failed.
The curtain of the sanctuary was split down the middle.
And Jesus called out with a loud voice,
"Father, into Your hands I entrust My spirit."
Saying this, He breathed His last. When the centurion saw
what happened, he began to glorify God, saying,
"This man really was righteous!"
Luke 23:44-47 HCSB

According to the *Holman Bible Dictionary*, a centurion was an officer in the Roman army who was over 100 soldiers. In Matthew 8:5 a centurion approached Jesus on behalf of his sick servant.

And when Jesus entered Capernaum, a centurion came to Him, imploring Him, and saying, "Lord, my servant is lying paralyzed at home, fearfully tormented." Jesus said to him, "I will come and heal him." But the centurion said, "Lord, I am not worthy for You to come under my roof, but just say the word, and my servant will be healed. "For I also am a man under authority, with soldiers under me; and I say to this one, 'Go!' and he goes, and to another, 'Come!' and he comes, and to my slave, 'Do this!' and he does it." Now when Jesus heard this, He marveled and said to those who were following, "Truly I say to you, I have not found such great faith with anyone in Israel. "I say to you that many will come from east and west, and recline at the table with Abraham, Isaac and Jacob in the kingdom of heaven; but the sons of the kingdom will be cast out into the outer darkness; in that place there will be weeping and gnashing of teeth." And Jesus said to the centurion, "Go; it shall be done for you as you have believed." And the servant was healed that very moment. (Matthew 8:5-13 NASB)

This centurion's faith was anchored on his understanding of authority. He understood that Jesus had authority to heal the sick. On another occasion a Pharisee begged Jesus to come to his house and put his hands on his daughter (Matthew 9:18), but this centurion believed that He just needed to speak the word. No wonder Jesus applauded his faith.

But for this centurion at the cross, there had to be something about Jesus that convicted his heart. Was it the way Jesus looked into his eyes when he pierced his hands with the nails? Was it the calm that bathed His face as the mob hurled their abuse? Was it what He didn't say and how He didn't yell back? Maybe it was the way the sky grew dark and the shutter of the earth that split the temple curtain in two. Whatever it was, this centurion was convinced, "This man really was righteous!"

Notice that anytime we proclaim truth the Bible says that we "glorify God." When we speak forth that which is true, we are bringing glory to God. Second Corinthians 1:20 is one of my favorite verses,

"For no matter how many promises God has made, they are 'Yes' in Christ."

That's my favorite part of the verse, but it's not all...

"...And so through Him [Jesus] the "Amen" [so be it] is spoken by us to the glory of God."

Did you get that part? All God's promises are YES, and when we choose to nail our confidence to those promises—when we stand on the dark side of the night and choose to ridiculously believe in the promises of God so thoroughly that we shout AMEN—*then* we bring glory to God.

The centurion watched Jesus take His final breath and shouted aloud, "surely He was the Son of God!" (Matthew 27:54). What will you shout when the sky is dark?

I'll Lead You to the Cross . . .

1. What promises are you waiting for God to fulfill?

2. How might you shout AMEN to the glory of God?

PRAY THIS PRAYER: *Lord, I believe that ALL Your promises are "YES!" Therefore I choose to say AMEN so that You might be glorified. Amen*

CHAPTER 93

MARY MAGDALENE

Many women were there looking on from a distance,
who had followed Jesus from Galilee while ministering to
Him. Among them was Mary Magdalene,
and Mary the mother of James and Joseph,
and the mother of the sons of Zebedee.
Matthew 27:55-56 NASB

Much fiction has been written with Mary of Magdala at the center of the story. Perhaps the most popular was the story that formed the basis of the controversial movie *The DaVinci Code*, starring Tom Hanks.

All we know from Scripture is that Mary Magdalene was a very sick woman before she met Jesus. According to Luke 8:2, Mary was tormented by seven demons. After Jesus healed her, she, along with other women, followed Him and ministered to His needs (and the needs of His disciples). Her motivation was gratitude for the life He'd restored to her.

And also some women who had been healed of evil spirits and sicknesses: Mary who was called Magdalene, from whom seven demons had gone out... (Luke 8:2 NASB)

Perhaps Mary's ministry included cooking, washing, and drawing water. Most likely Mary supported Jesus' ministry financially. She also followed Him to Jerusalem on this fateful trip. I personally have a very hard time picturing these women at the cross. To think that their devotion pressed them on! It was not an easy journey.

And following Him was a large crowd of the people, and of women who were mourning and lamenting Him. But Jesus turning to them said, "Daughters of Jerusalem, stop weeping for Me, but weep for yourselves and for your children. For behold, the days are coming when they will say, 'Blessed are the barren, and the wombs that never bore, and the breasts that never nursed.'" (Luke 23:27-29 NASB)

And although Jesus spoke to them on the way, they continued their trek until they knelt at the foot of the cross. What amazing women to be there at the cross! They weren't afraid of the Jewish rulers. They didn't care if the violence made them sick. Out of love for Jesus they continued their ministry to Him this time simply by their presence.

Don't you love how women minister to one another? I have a friend; her name is Kathleen. Last week I received devastating news, the kind of news that makes your world stop spinning. I called Kathleen and asked her to assemble my prayer partners (I have seven loyal women who pray for me daily). I told her my news but asked her to keep the details vague when she shared it with the others. Sometimes the crises we encounter warrant confidentiality. This was one of those times.

Before the week was over, Kathleen had assembled my prayer warriors, made reservations at a hotel, cancelled those reservations, purchased groceries (including toilet paper that I desperately needed but didn't think to include on the list), walked at least 14 miles with me while I worked through my confusion, took me to lunch, reminded me of a task that needed completing, and handed me a pack of Kleenex just before worship with the warning, "You're going to need these today."

I love how women minister to one another! I honestly don't know if I would have survived that week without Kathleen. I thank God for Mary Magdalene and the ministry she offered to Jesus. I thank God for the Mary Magdalenes who are ministering in His Name today.

I'LL LEAD YOU TO THE CROSS . . .

1. Who has ministered to you like Mary Magdalene? Take time to write her a thank you note.

2. Who might you minister to today?

PRAY THIS PRAYER: *Father, thank You for the ministry of women like Mary Magdalene. Help me to be a woman like that. I want to be aware of and quick to respond to the physical and spiritual needs of those You put in my path today. Amen*

CHAPTER 94

JOHN, THE BELOVED

When Jesus saw his mother there, and the disciple whom he
loved standing nearby, he said to his mother,
"Dear woman, here is your son."
And to the disciple, "Here is your mother."
From that time on, this disciple took her into his home."
John 19:26-27

In his gospel, John consistently referred to himself as "the disciple whom [Jesus] loved."

At the Last Supper: *"One of them, the disciple whom Jesus loved, was reclining next to him."* (John 13:23)

Then again at the breakfast on the beach: *"Peter turned and saw that the disciple whom Jesus loved was following them."* (John 21:20)

Isn't that a great statement of John's faith? He was so convinced that Jesus *loved him* that he called himself "the disciple whom Jesus loved."

One of the first songs I ever remember singing was this one: *Jesus loves me, this I know, for the Bible tells me so. Little ones to Him belong, they are weak but He is strong.*

Yes, Jesus loves me! Yes, Jesus loves me. Yes, Jesus loves me! The Bible tells me so.

My father sat next to me on the piano bench and taught me how to play it on the piano. When I grew older, I learned the sign language and Spanish versions. If you were fortunate enough to grow up with a rich spiritual heritage, you no doubt know this song too.

I've lived long enough to realize that there are times that this is all I know.

Jesus loves me this I know...

...like the time a couple in our church lost their baby on Christmas Day; the time when I held the baby of a young mother while we buried her; the time I heard my own daughter say "I'm going to do this my way!" knowing deep in my spirit that her way was going to lead her down a path she didn't want to go; the time a trusted friend called my husband a liar; that day my doctor told me I had cancer...my list could go on and on. There are so many times when the Enemy shakes our world but when our faith is anchored on the unshakable love of Jesus we can sing.

John knew he was loved by Jesus. Do you?

"Jesus loves me this I *know*."

I'LL LEAD YOU TO THE CROSS . . .

1. When has Jesus' love been all you've known?

2. How has the love of Jesus sustained you?

PRAY THIS PRAYER: *Thank You, Jesus, for loving me. Let me have the rock solid understanding that John had. Let me know I am the one whom You love. Amen*

CHAPTER 95

MARY
THE MOTHER OF JESUS

*Standing by the cross of Jesus were His mother, His mother's
sister, Mary the wife of Clopas, and Mary Magdalene.
When Jesus saw His mother and the disciple He loved
standing there, He said to His mother, "Woman, here is
your son." Then He said to the disciple,
"Here is your mother." And from that hour
the disciple took her into his home.*
John 19:25-27 HCSB

I wrote a story about Mary's presence at the cross. It is
published in my book *Women Touched by Jesus*. But it
warrants repeating here. So for the next few days we
will sit at the cross with Mary.

She felt something warm splash on her neck then
trickle down her back, but the pain in her heart far out-
weighed any other sensation. The ground was rough and
full of rocks that cut into her shins as she desperately tried
to bow herself low and absorb the reality of this day. She
rhythmically bumped her forehead against the splinter-
filled rugged wood in an effort to give some sort of desperate expression to her indescribable pain.

"Aaaaauuuu!" Oh how she longed to cry out. But there were not sounds deep enough to give voice to her sorrow. So instead of opening her mouth, she drug her now bleeding knees even closer to where the soldiers had thumped that post into the ground. She wrapped her gentle arms around that Roman symbol of authority and shame and didn't even notice when the splinters dug into her soft hands.

It was as close to her dying son as she could get.

Mary did you know? That little boy would one day be a king.

"No, I didn't know. I didn't know I'd be here today."

Mary was unaware of the others around her. Their mocking didn't have any effect on her. She was all alone at the cross that day. And though her body knelt where His blood spilled, Mary was far, far away. It was late in the morning, and she was only 15.

"Greetings to you who are highly favored! The Lord is with you!"

What did He mean by that? Mary remembered the day that changed everything. She remembered the innocent wonder. She smiled again at Gabriel's calm assurance that the power of the Most High God would overshadow her. Mary remembered.

"Oh God, Most High…I desperately need the power of your Holy Spirit to overshadow me this instant!"

Mary heard a noise…"Oh Jesus, don't try to talk, it

won't be long now and You'll be back where You belong! Oh Jesus…" She looked up at His face. He bent His head so that His swollen bloodshot eyes were gazing into hers and in a gurgling whisper He said,

"Dear woman, here is your son." As He forced the words out of His collapsing chest, He glanced over toward John.

"What? Where? You are my Son, dear Jesus…bleeding and dying Oh God, I need You now!" Mary's pain was more than she could bear.

Jesus was motioning to His dearly loved friend and disciple, John. John's own face was filled with torment. But he caught the meaning of his Master's words, and immediately John came to Mary. He nodded understanding and wrapped his arms around her trembling shoulders. When John did this, Jesus nodded slowly and almost whispered again in a guttural noise, "Here is your mother," He said to John.

I'LL LEAD YOU TO THE CROSS . . .

1. Remember how God protected Mary and provided graciously for her in the early months of her pregnancy? He sent her to Elizabeth where she found security and joy. Just as God protected her then, so He was still providing for her now. Consider how God does the same for you.

2. Have you ever walked through something you couldn't imagine surviving? How did God provide for you in that situation?

PRAY THIS PRAYER: *Lord, I thank You that You never ask anything of us that we can't do. Thank You that You provide enough grace to take care of our every need. Amen*

CHAPTER 96

DISCOURAGEMENT AND GRIEF

He has filled the hungry with good things
but has sent the rich away empty.
Luke 1:53

The story of Mary continued:

"Thank You, Lord. Even as You die…You're meeting my every need." Mary wondered at how God could be so attentive. With the strength of John's shared grief, Mary was once again far away in her thoughts. She remembered how full of joy and wonder she was when she responded to Gabriel's message,

"I am the Lord's servant, may it be to me as you have said."

How could she have possibly known that commitment would cost her so? Even after he'd spoken, Mary remembered how the reality of Gabriel's words began to soak in, and how afraid she was to tell her mother and father about her pregnancy. Would they understand? What would she do? Mary remembered how Mama suggested she go visit Elizabeth and see for herself this miracle pregnancy Gabriel told her about. If Elizabeth were pregnant, then what Gabriel said had to be true. The family knew of Elizabeth's bareness, and no woman (save Sarah) conceived and gave birth at such an age!

Oh, she would never forget Elizabeth's greeting: "Blessed are you among women!" Mary remembered how blessed she felt; she responded to Elizabeth by shouting, "my soul glorifies the Lord and my spirit rejoices in God my Savior!"

And did she ever rejoice! It was at Elizabeth's home that the full impact of God's choosing her began to envelop her with wonder. God was bringing the promised Messiah, and He was bringing Him as a baby—her baby. Mary smiled at the memory of those gentle days...the days before life became so complicated. Neither she nor Elizabeth had any clue what their partnership with God would demand of them.

"Oh God, thank You for Elizabeth's faith. What grace she demonstrated when You took John from her!"

Another splash of crimson liquid on her neck, and the warmth of the trickle abruptly interrupted her moment of reflection as it ran down her back.

"Oh God, how can this be?" Mary wondered. She realized His very life was dripping away.

Mary remembered the night He was born. The pregnancy had been amazing. After her sickness went away, she lay awake at night talking to Him as she felt Him move in her womb. She wondered how God could do something so amazing and choose her to be part of it. She thanked God again and again for trusting her with such a task. Mary remembered how gentle Joseph was. A pang of grief stabbed her already heavy heart as she recalled his death. Joseph was always the gentle, good provider, lover, and friend. They were partners together in this. Mary couldn't have survived Jesus' birth without him. She smiled as she remembered how he'd taken care of all the details while she suffered the pains of labor. She remembered how Joseph shook with wonder when he presented her with the precious bundle of holiness. She remembered how the two of them counted His fingers and toes in those first few hours when they were all alone with Him in that stable. Thank You, Lord, for Joseph.

Mary remembered how He'd nursed at her very own breast. She peeled her arms from the rugged cross and pressed them to her breast while John shifted to make room for her to move.

"Jesus…I nursed You!" "Oh God…"

I'LL LEAD YOU TO THE CROSS . . .

1. Pause for a moment at the cross with Mary. Think of what it must have been to nurse Jesus.

2. Do you have a son? If you do, do you think you could have watched him be crucified? Just a thought to ponder...

PRAY THIS PRAYER: *As I read this story, Lord, I'm reminded that following You is not easy. Thank You for the joy in my life. And when I face various trials, help me to discover the "pure joy" that's there too. I want to be like Mary, strong enough to "be there" when life grows dark. Amen*

CHAPTER 97

CONFUSION AND PROMISES

He has performed mighty deeds with is arm; he has scattered those who are proud in their inmost thoughts.

Luke 1:51

The story of Mary continued:

Mary looked up at His feet. He was shifting them in search for some sort of relief from the suffocating pressure filling His lungs with fluid as He hung on that cross. Those feet, those precious feet. Mary remembered cuddling His feet. He loved to have His toes tickled. She remembered when He took His first step and how He laughed when He toddled all the way from her arms to the arms of Joseph stretched out to hold Him.

Oh, the places those feet had been. She stretched her hand up the cross in an attempt to press her fingertips to His toes, but they hung just out of her reach. Two other times she hadn't been able to reach Him. The time He gave them such a fright when He stayed behind at the temple, talking with the Pharisees. She remembered how frantic she was when she thought they'd lost Him. She remembered the fears that pressed against her heart when she looked and looked but couldn't find Him anywhere among family and friends that day. Then she remembered how amazed she was when she stood at the edge of the circle of religious leaders who were captivated by Him as He taught the teachers in the temple. And she wondered how a 12-year-old boy could be so wise.

Mary also remembered the other time she couldn't reach Him. Once again she felt the twinge of hurt when she'd heard Him say, "behold my mother and my brothers! For whoever does the will of my Father in heaven is my brother and sister and mother." She'd known from the beginning that He was not hers. But hers was a unique role. She fed and clothed Him, rocked and bathed Him. She spent hours talking and listening to Him. She knew He was God's Son, and that she was God's partner in bringing Him here.

The sky grew unusually dark. Mary didn't notice the people that fell in fear all around her. She didn't hear the Roman soldiers whisper. She didn't sense any of the oppression others seemed to sense. Mary turned her eyes toward the heavens and listened for God to speak to her once again.

Mary remembered His laughter. She remembered His tears. She remembered how He loved without fear and how He always responded to people with kindness and compassion. She saw snapshots of Him turning water into wine. She could almost hear the festivities of the wedding. She saw Him baptized and thought for a moment she caught the flutter of dove's wings flapping in the wind. Mary heard the Pharisees accusations as they confronted Him on so many occasions. She observed the weariness she saw in His eyes when the crowds followed Him even as He sought to go away and rest. She saw Him glance at her as He told the disciples another parable.

For three hours Mary knelt at the foot of the cross and heard His voice—she saw His face. She never once saw Him grimace or heard Him complain.

Gabriel's words echoed in her ears… "He will reign over the house of Jacob forever; his kingdom will never end."

"How can this be? This cross is definitely an end to Jesus' life. Did something go wrong?" Mary felt another splash of His warm blood on the back of her neck as Jesus hung silently suspended between earth and heaven just above her head.

"What did You mean, Lord? The shepherds said the angels sang! 'Glory to God in the highest and peace on earth'…were we too corrupt to embrace Your peace?" Mary wondered, and the sky grew darker.

I'LL LEAD YOU TO THE CROSS . . .

1. When you are confused, go back to the promises God gave you long ago. Camp out on them. Understand that when God gave them to you, He already knew this day would come.

2. Thank God that all His promises are "yes!"

PRAY THIS PRAYER: *Father, sometimes I don't understand. I don't understand why bad things happen; I don't understand why there's so much suffering, and I don't understand why everyone doesn't know You like I do. Help me to trust Your Word when I don't understand. Amen*

CHAPTER 98

PUTTING THE PIECES TOGETHER

My soul glorifies the Lord and my spirit rejoices in God my Savior, for he has been mindful of the humble state of his servant. From now on all generations will call me blessed.

Luke 1:46-48

The story of Mary continued:

Then, a cloud began to lift in Mary's heart. In her mind, she heard Jesus speak as she pondered the things He taught: "If anyone would come after Me, he must deny himself and take up his cross daily and follow Me."

What did this cross have to do with His kingdom?

"For God so loved the world that He gave His one and only Son that whoever believes in Him shall not perish but have eternal life. For God did not send His Son into the world to condemn the world but to save the world through Him."

"Eternal life...He taught about life in heaven with His Father. A different life, a life beyond the grave. He came that we might have life...abundant life He called it." Mary wondered at these words, "I am the resurrection and the life."

"He healed the sick, made the lame walk again. He gave sight to the blind and opened deaf ears. He brought people back from the dead. If His death was not part of God's plan, He wouldn't be dying. He certainly had power over life and death! Jesus chose to hang on that cross. It was the Father's plan!"

Mary slowly rose to stand. She'd been bent down so long that her legs shook as she unfolded them and stepped back from the foot of the cross. She looked up at the dying body of her beloved Jesus and again she heard these words, "My heart is troubled and what shall I say, 'Father, save me from this hour?' No, it was for this very reason I came to this hour. Father glorify Your name!"

"This is why He came! This is why God brought Him here! Behold the Lamb of God, who takes away the sins of the world! He is bearing the weight of our guilt and shame. He is dying so we can live! He is taking on the sins of the world!"

Understanding welled up in Mary's soul. She stumbled and fell again to her knees, "He's taking on my sin too." Mary thought about her life before Gabriel greeted her that day, and of how even in her innocent youth she too felt the desperate need for a Savior. Mary longed for a bridge between her own heart and the heart of God. Mary remembered how she'd fallen short plenty of times from the holiness of God as a child and as an adult. She realized that the way to the Father was through His Son.

"For God so loved the world that He gave His only begotten Son, Jesus to die for *me*! God gave Jesus through me and for me!" Mary thanked God for sending Jesus to make the way for her and so many others to come to Him.

A tiny smile formed on her lips when Mary's wonder was interrupted by Jesus' loud shout. Unlike the other words He'd spoken from the cross, this time His voice was loud and vibrant with the same authority that had astounded the rulers and set the captives free.

"It is Finished!"

I'LL LEAD YOU TO THE CROSS . . .

1. Read again Mary's song of praise in Luke 1:46-55.

2. What song has God given you to sing?

PRAY THIS PRAYER: *Thank You, Lord, for calling us when we're young and naïve. Thank You for growing us gradually into the harder parts of following You. Help me to sing every day even when I'm grieving. Amen*

CHAPTER 99

SURRENDER

"I am the Lord's servant," Mary answered,
"May it be to me as you have said."

Luke 1:38

The story of Mary continued:

A tiny smile had formed on her lips when Mary's wonder was interrupted by Jesus' loud shout. Unlike the other words He'd spoken from the cross, this time His voice was loud and vibrant with the same authority that had astounded the rulers and set the captives free.

"It is finished!" And then He breathed His last.

Silence. There was complete…penetrating silence.

Mary sat still for a moment then lifted her head to look around her. For the first time, she noticed the people who were at the cross with her. So many people were lost and confused. Most of the chief priests and scribes had long ago left. Simon, the traveler who'd carried His cross, stood solemn with his arms draped around two small boys. The disciples were shaking with grief-huddled over to the side. And many others just stared up at His body. The hope they had seemed to hang onto was dead on that cross. Even the Pharisees who remained looked shaken and afraid. They didn't understand what had just happened. Everyone's eyes reflected pain and desperation. They felt like she did when she first knelt there.

Mary was not sure what to do next, but she sensed some sort of supernatural peace flooding her broken heart. She rubbed her hand behind her neck and drew her palms close to her face so that she could examine His blood she wiped from there. In a silent prayer of deep sorrow mingled with incredible gratitude and undeniable peace, she remembered how this had all begun.

Most people might have thought that it began in the garden yesterday evening. Some of His disciples might trace events back to the triumphal entry the week before. The Jewish leaders most likely marked the beginning when they met in Caiaphas' home. But this day didn't begin this morning...not last night...not even when Judas chose to sell Him out.

Mary remembered the day as if it were today. Gabriel greeted her with his unusual salutation, "Greetings, you who are highly favored! The Lord is with you."

She remembered her total trust and dependence on God. The excitement of her visit with Elizabeth and the joy in which she sang her song. "My soul glorifies the Lord and my spirit rejoices in God my Savior!"

And with the memory of that greeting from Gabriel and that visit with Elizabeth flooding her mind and heart, she prayed again..."I am still Your servant, Lord. Be it done to me as You have said."

I'll Lead You to the Cross . . .

1. What about you—can you do that? Can you suffer deeply and still surrender?

2. Ask God to link your heart intimately, powerfully with His. Tell Him you trust Him with your whole heart.

Pray this prayer: *"I am still Your servant Lord. Be it done to me as You have said."* Amen

CHAPTER 100

IT IS FINISHED!

When He had received the drink, Jesus said, "It is finished."
With that, he bowed his head and gave up his spirit.

John 19:30

IT IS FINISHED.

Three of the most powerful words in Scripture. Jesus had been mocked, spit on, and beat with fists, hit with reeds, whipped with the cat of nine tails. His beard had been plucked from His face, a crown of thorns pressed into His head. He'd been heckled, falsely accused, convicted, and nailed to a cross. His pain was so real that His death was relief. But none of what He'd suffered physically could even begin to compare to the separation He'd experienced when He became sin for us.

When Jesus said, "It is finished," the wrath of God was satisfied. The penalty for your sin was PAID IN FULL. No matter how horrible it was, how sorry you are, or even how many times you did it, Jesus took care of its POWER to hold you captive when He died on that cross!!

We are no better than the chief priests and scribes when we refuse to forgive ourselves for the mistakes we've made. In essence we are telling God that what Jesus did on the cross was not enough—that there was more He should have done to cover our particular sin. If that had been so, Jesus wouldn't have declared it FINISHED.

So how do we break free from the shame, regret, and confusion of our sin? Confess your sin to God. Receive His forgiveness in full, and get help if you need it to break your sin habit.

Jesus forgives sin. And what is even better, God refuses to hold your sin against you. He promises that when you confess your sin He will never bring it up again—ever.

Therefore, there is now no condemnation for those who are in Christ Jesus, because through Christ Jesus the law of the Spirit of life set me free from the law of sin and death. (Romans 8:1-2)

Your Enemy will try to convince you that Jesus' death was not enough—that there is more you have to do to overcome your mistakes; or that you've out-sinned the sacrifice of Christ. Know that this simply is not so. If you are hearing a voice telling you to repent, it's the voice of conviction—confess your sin.

If we confess our sins, he is faithful and just and will forgive us our sins and purify us from all unrighteousness. (1 John 1:9)

If that voice is mocking you, then tell it to cease, for Jesus declared you redeemed.

I'LL LEAD YOU TO THE CROSS . . .

1. What past mistakes or current habits do you struggle with?

2. How does knowing Jesus paid for your sin completely help you cope with those things?

PRAY THIS PRAYER: *Lord, I am sorry for {whatever sin or habit aggravates you}. I humbly ask You to forgive me for {whatever you did}. I realize that Jesus died for this sin too. I receive Your forgiveness. I renounce the thoughts that plague me with shame. I profess that I am beautiful, clean, and pure before You. And I am free to be a productive disciple of Christ through the power of Your Holy Spirit working in and through me. Thank You for the cross, Lord. Amen*

MEET ME AT THE MANGER ...
AND I'LL LEAD YOU
TO THE CROSS